A Necessary Order

Don Bogen

Theodore Roethke and the Writing Process

Ohio University Press

Athens

PS
3535
.039
Z586
1991

/ 5 8903
may 1993

96   95   94   93   92   91   5   4   3   2   1

Ohio University Press books are printed on acid-free paper ∞

Library of Congress Cataloging-in-Publication Data

Bogen, Don.
    A necessary order: Theodore Roethke and the writing process / Don
Bogen.
        p.   cm.
    Includes bibliographical references (p.   ) and index.
    ISBN 0-8214-0975-1
    1. Roethke, Theodore, 1908-1963—Criticism and interpretation.
I. Title.
PS3535.039Z586   1991
811'.54—dc20   90-7985
                                                                    CIP

In Memory of Josephine Miles

CONTENTS

ACKNOWLEDGMENTS

The Theodore Roethke Papers have been the central resource for this book. I would like to thank Beatrice Roethke Lushington for her permission to work with this unpublished material, and for her encouragement and valuable comments. The staff of the Roethke Collection at the Suzallo Library, University of Washington, were a great help in my research. Grants from the University of California Department of English, the University of Cincinnati Research Council, and the University of Cincinnati Charles Phelps Taft Memorial Fund made the research possible. I would like to thank Marilyn Schwiers for typing the manuscript and Holly Panich and the staff at Ohio University Press for seeing it through publication. I am grateful to the editors of *English Literary History* and *Papers on Language and Literature* for their permission to reprint material from my articles "From *Open House* to the Greenhouse: Theodore Roethke's Poetic Breakthrough" (ELH, Summer, 1980) and " 'Intuition' and 'Craftsmanship': Theodore Roethke at Work" (PLL, Winter, 1982).

Various people have seen different parts of this book and provided helpful criticism. I am especially grateful to Peter Manning, James Breslin, Gerald Mendelsohn, Alex Zwerdling, Walter Pavlich, Marjorie Perloff, Arnold Stein, Ralph J. Mills, Jr., and Jenijoy La Belle. I have also benefited from conversations with Roethke's former students Tess Gallagher and the late Richard Hugo. I would like to thank Paul Alpers for his help at the beginning of the project and my colleagues James K. Robinson, Hugh Staples, and Nancy Lenz Harvey for their encouragement and support. To the late Josephine Miles—poet, scholar, and teacher—I owe my deepest gratitude.

CHAPTER ONE

Introduction

When I first began working with the Theodore Roethke Papers at the University of Washington, I was reminded of Roethke's comment about his father's greenhouse: "It was a jungle, and it was paradise."[1] This enormous collection includes over two hundred fifty notebooks, more than eight thousand pages of loose notes, extensive draft material for practically all Roethke's poems, reams of incoming and outgoing correspondence, plus teaching notes, copies of other poets' work in Roethke's hand, and a welter of memorabilia. For scholars and poets the potential of this material is overwhelming. The challenge comes in trying to make sense of it. Roethke's notebooks are the heart of this "jungle." Paging through a few at random to get a feel for the poet's working method, I was astounded by their chaotic intensity. Lines of prose and poetry in different ink sprawl across the pages, sometimes covering older material or jutting out perpendicular to the margins. Fragmentary drafts of letters and talks, poems and parts of poems by writers from the Renaissance to the twentieth century, reading notes, and personal reminders are interspersed throughout. Erratic dating shows Roethke's frequent re-reading of the notebooks, and lines and passages everywhere are crossed out, crayoned over, or circled for consideration. Coming through all this confusion is a presence not seen on the neat pages of Roethke's *Collected Poems*. The notebooks, drafts, and other unpublished material provide a glimpse of the poet literally at work. In this book I want to illuminate that presence by examining the process of writing itself, how it evolved over the course of Roethke's career and what it meant to the poet.

In *Alone with America* Richard Howard identifies process as a central motif in contemporary poetry. Poets as diverse as John Ashbery and Robert Bly, Anthony Hecht and Robert Creeley, come together in their desire to "address themselves to the current, to the flux, to the process of experience rather than to its precepts."[2] Though part of an earlier generation, Roethke is no exception here. As Richard Blessing shows in *Theodore Roethke's Dynamic Vision*, Roethke saw the world as something constantly in motion and tried to reflect this essential dynamism in his work.[3] The resulting poems, particularly those in Roethke's sequences, often seem more process than product. The process I am studying is not the one embodied in the finished text but that which precedes it, the generation of poetic material and its revision and arrangement into its final form. This process, I believe, can reveal aspects of both the text and the poet which might otherwise have remained hidden.

A basic assumption behind my study is that textual changes made in the writing process do not reflect aesthetic choices alone. I suspect this assumption is valid for most poets' work, but it is especially true in Roethke's case. In his letters and essays Roethke is perceptive and articulate about the technical aspects of writing, particularly aural effects, but he rarely discusses craft in a vacuum. Roethke worked hard to perfect his poems, often revising right up to the moment of publication and sometimes after, but his overall goals in writing were not aesthetic alone; art involved more than the perfection of artifacts. As he put it in a seminar on identity at Northwestern University:

> The human problem is to find out what one really *is*: whether one exists, whether existence is possible. But how? (SP 20, Roethke's emphasis).

Looking at the poet in the process of writing, I hope to shed some light on how Roethke dealt with the problem of personal identity.

When I first started working with the Roethke Papers, I was looking for clear links between specific poems and events in Roethke's life. This approach is appropriate for some poets. Yeats' journal, for instance, shows many poems arising out of specific incidents with Maud Gonne, Lady Gregory, or the Abbey Theater, and Yeats himself confirmed this close relation between poetry and daily life when he wrote that he really found himself in poetry only when he set out not to produce deliberately beautiful work "but merely to lighten the mind of some burden of love or bitterness thrown upon it by the events of life."[4] But for Roethke, the relation between poetry and "the events of life" is considerably less direct. Specific biographical details, though interesting, offer few connections to developments in the work. Allan Seager's *The Glass House: The Life of Theodore Roethke* covers these details extensively. Along with Roethke's own letters and prose pieces, this biography gives a good overall sense of the poet's life. Roethke was born in Saginaw, Michigan in 1908; grew up there; attended the University of Michigan and Harvard; held various teaching positions at Lafayette College, Michigan State, Pennsylvania State, Bennington, and the University of Washington; married his former student Beatrice O'Connell in 1953; won the Pulitzer Prize and the National Book Award; and died of a heart attack in 1963.[5]

These "events of life" do not illuminate Roethke's work or even appear much in the poems. Rather, Roethke's poetry reveals certain focal points in his past, most importantly his father, the greenhouse the father owned and managed, and the father's death in 1923 when Roethke was fourteen. The intense relation between the poet and his father is central to Roethke's poetry, particularly his experimental, autobiographical work of the 1940s. Undoubtedly this complex relation has something to do with the periodic mental breakdowns Roethke suffered during his life. Rosemary Sullivan's *Theodore Roethke: The Garden Master* and Karl Malkoff's *Theodore Roethke: An Introduction to the Poetry* both trace the psychological tensions that appear in Roethke's work. Other critics have looked specifically at the breakdowns for clues to Roethke's poetry. Allan Seager speculates in some detail about the pattern of Roethke's breakdowns, and Neal Bowers sees a link between the poet's manic-depressive tendencies and mysticism in *Theodore Roethke: The Journey from I to Otherwise*. Though bouts of mental illness were a part of Roethke's life, it is important not to over-emphasize this aspect of his character. The idea of the poet as mad genius is a seductive myth at least as old as Romanticism. It has little relevance to Roethke, as even a quick look at the material the poet wrote during his stays in the hospital shows: when he was mad, Roethke wrote nothing of value. Much of Roethke's poetry examines the irrational and unconscious sides of the self, but this powerful work did not arise from specific breakdowns. If anything, it was developed in spite of these debilitating episodes.

For my purposes, developments in Roethke's writing are considerably more important than events in his life. The poet's career divides readily into three periods, corresponding roughly to the decades in which he was writing. Each period has particular styles and kinds of poems associated with it, and the differences between periods reflect significant changes in the way Roethke went about writing and what the process meant to him. Roethke's early period dates from the early '30s, in which he first began to write seriously, to the publication of his first volume, *Open House*, in 1941.[6] The work of this period is largely formal, abstract, and impersonal. For the young poet, writing involved the development of an essentially artificial sense of identity; the process of composition was one of self-creation. Roethke's eventual dissatisfaction with this kind of work led to an important breakthrough in the vivid greenhouse poems of the early '40s and the sequences of multi-sectioned poems which followed them. The two volumes of Roethke's middle period, *The Lost Son and Other Poems* in 1948 and *Praise to the End!* in 1951, include the poet's most experimental and intensely personal work. The writing process has changed from a kind of self-creation to genuine self-discovery, with the poet devising radically new techniques to generate material from memory and the unconscious. Roethke's last period, from 1951 until his death in 1963, is characterized by what he termed "the long journey out of the self" ("Journey to the Interior," 1. 1). This movement outward, away from concentration on problems of identity, surfaces in Roethke's new interest in the formal love poem as well as his development of the two major sequences of this period, *Meditations of an Old Woman* in the mid-'50s and *North American Sequence* in the late '50s and early '60s. Roethke published two volumes of new and selected poems in his last period; *The Waking: Poems 1933-1953* in 1954 and *Words for the Wind* in 1957; his last volume, *The Far Field,* appeared posthumously in 1964. The three stages in Roethke's career show a basic pattern of achievement, followed by reaction against the achievement and a corresponding new way of writing. An identity created through writing in the early work is eventually seen as artificial and replaced with the concept of writing as self-discovery in Roethke's middle period; this immersion in self, in its turn, becomes a limitation which the poet seeks to escape in his last period.

    This book follows the developments in Roethke's career chronologically. Since my interest is in the process of writing, I do not intend to discuss all of the poet's work or provide a critical interpretation of each major poem. This has already been done by Malkoff and Sullivan, as well as Jay Parini in *Theodore Roethke: An American Romantic,* and to discuss how every poem was *written* would, of course, take volumes. Rather, I shall be focussing on the poems and groups of poems which show the overall developments in the writing process most clearly. Because the problem of identity is at the heart of the creative process, my analysis of Roethke's poems—especially those of his middle period—involves a close look at particular facets of the material, including the psychosexual associations of images, the personal implications of changes in style and poetic voice, the role of memory and the unconscious, and the way poetic structures parallel Roethke's psychic development. I do not mean to suggest by this that Roethke wrote only about the self or that his poems can only be interpreted in relation to his changing sense of identity. As Roethke noted, identity was "the human problem" for him, and it is central to developments in the writing process; but there are, of course, many other sides to his work which cannot be discussed in this study.

Because both what Roethke wrote and the way he wrote changed greatly over the course of his career, the major chapters in this book approach the material from different angles, relying on different kinds of evidence from the Roethke Papers. My study begins in Chapter 2 with a discussion of the process of self-creation Roethke undertook as he met the challenge of a first volume. Here I want to take a close look at the concept of self announced in the title poem of *Open House* and consider some important factors in the volume's gradual evolution: poems excluded from it and the reasons for their exclusion, Roethke's developing feelings about the work, and comments from the poet's friends and associates. Chapter 3 then examines the breakthrough Roethke made after the publication of his first volume by analyzing the composition of three representative poems: one written in the mid-'30s, a transitional work from the late '30s, and one of the greenhouse poems from the early '40s. The writing process changed radically at this point in Roethke's career, as a comparison of notebook work, drafts, and techniques of revision shows. The most important development of Roethke's middle period is his construction of the four-poem "Lost Son" sequence in his second volume and, later, the larger sequence which incorporates these four poems in *Praise to the End!* Chapter 4 examines the cyclic process behind Roethke's composition and arrangement of the two sequences, discussing these autobiographical poems in their order of composition and their relation to problems of personal identity. Chapter 5 then looks in detail at the composition of one of these poems, in which we can see Roethke's writing methods at their most complex and intense as he attempts to expand the process of self-discovery through the liberation of unconscious material. The last two major chapters of my study focus on Roethke's final period. Chapter 6 considers the first development in Roethke's drive to move beyond the limitations of the self: the formal love poem. In looking at the ways the different love poems are related and the new techniques used to develop these pieces, I want to show how Roethke gradually clarified his feelings and began to reach outward toward union with another. Chapter 7 examines the poet's clearest formulation of "the long journey out of the self" in the two major sequences of his last period. The changes in the process of composition between these sequences and those of the middle period are significant here, as is Roethke's development of the central metaphor of the journey; both reveal the growth of a new approach to writing and the self.

Studying how Roethke went about writing, I have benefited greatly from the work of Roethke's friends, students, critics, and especially fellow poets. The poets Louise Bogan, W. H. Auden, Stanley Kunitz, and William Carlos Williams all knew Roethke as a man and a poet, and their comments in reviews, letters, and interviews have special value. *Theodore Roethke: Essays on the Poetry,* edited by Arnold Stein, a former colleague of Roethke at the University of Washington, has been essential. Roethke's students, including James Wright, Carolyn Kizer, Richard Hugo, and Tess Gallagher, have made revealing comments on Roethke and the process of writing in letters, interviews, essays, and conversation; and Jenijoy La Belle, a student in Roethke's last class, has done perceptive work on the poet's literary ancestors in *The Echoing Wood of Theodore Roethke.* It seems appropriate for a study of the writing process that most of those who are cited in this book are themselves poets, including the critics Richard Blessing, Neal Bowers, and Jay Parini, and figures as diverse as William Meredith, Stephen Spender, John Crowe Ransom, and Seamus Heaney.

My most important resource has been Roethke himself. I have made use of David Wagoner's selections from Roethke's notebooks in *Straw for the Fire,* as well as the two works edited by Ralph J. Mills, Jr.: the poet's *Selected Letters* (abbreviated "SL" in my citations) and *On the Poet and His Craft: Selected Prose of Theodore Roethke* (abbreviated "SP"). My text for finished poems, unless otherwise noted, is *The Collected Poems of Theodore Roethke.* In quoting from the longer poems I give first the section number, followed by a period and the line numbers. The main source of material on the process of writing is the Theodore Roethke Papers themselves.[7] In citing this unpublished work, I use the abbreviation "TR" and list first the box number and then the folder number within the box. As there are no folders in the boxes of Roethke's notebooks, the second figure in this case is the actual notebook number.

Roethke's own interest in analyzing the writing process dates from the beginning of his career. In the essay "Verse in Rehearsal," published in 1939, he discusses some of the revisions in his poem "Genesis," concluding, "Of course these changes are only a crude representation of one stage in the making of a poem. A far better way to study this problem is to work with original manuscripts or facsimiles" (SP 35). With the Theodore Roethke Papers at hand, we can follow the poet's advice.

"Myself Is What I Wear":
Self-Creation in *Open House*

Looking back at his first volume, *Open House,* fourteen years after its publication, Theodore Roethke complained, "It took me ten years to complete one little book, and now some of the things in it seem to creak. Still, I like about ten pieces in it" (SP 16). Roethke's harsh judgment, I think, reflects not only his sense of his own progress in the craft of verse but also an essential dissatisfaction with the vision of self presented in *Open House.* The beginning and title poem of the volume gives a basic statement of this vision. In this chapter I want to define the sense of self in "Open House" and then consider how it evolved in the composition of the book as a whole. Two parts of the writing process are especially revealing here: Roethke's development of the five sections of *Open House* and his selection of poems for the volume. In his choice of material for the book and his arrangement of it, we can see Roethke essentially creating an identity as he completes his first volume.

A first book presents a special challenge for any poet; and for Roethke, who was known for his extreme concern with literary success, the challenge was formidable. Though Roethke had been publishing poems in prestigious magazines like *The New Yorker* and *The New Republic* since the early '30s, *Open House* was not accepted for publication until 1940, when the poet was thirty-one. It appeared a year later in the spring of 1941. Roethke's letters of the late '30s show his increasing anxiety about the volume as the years went by. He complained to his friend Louise Bogan that he still had no book out on his twenty-eighth birthday (SL 37), and as the publishers' rejections came in he became increasingly upset, at one point going so far as to draft a

rather angry reply to the editor who turned him down at Macmillan (TR
16–4). While he was sending out the volume in the late '30s he continued to work on both individual poems and the structure of the book as
a whole, relying heavily on detailed correspondence with Bogan,
Stanley Kunitz, Rolfe Humphries, and other poets. As many critics
have noted, Roethke served a long and conscientious poetic
apprenticeship.

In *Theodore Roethke's Dynamic Vision*, Richard Blessing argues
that *Open House* is essentially an apprentice work, for which Roethke
selected what he considered his best poems, those, according to Blessing, which were most "intense."[1] Roethke clearly was something of a
beginner in his first book, and Blessing's idea of the process of selection is a natural view of the way a young poet might go about the task
of assembling a first volume. But I think there is a bit more involved
than mere selection of the best works in Roethke's case. For one thing,
Roethke rejected more than a dozen poems whose literary merit had
been clearly certified by their publication in journals like *Poetry, The
Sewanee Review, The Atlantic,* and *The New Yorker*; he also excluded
the poem "River Incident" from the book, even though he thought it
good enough to include in *The Lost Son and Other Poems* seven years
later. His frequent rearrangements of the poems within the sections of
the book and the order of the sections themselves also suggest that
Open House was more than a gathering of the best poems he had written. Unlike an established poet, the beginning writer must put together
a volume which not only communicates that the work is good but also
that the poet, though young, is important and worth reading. A first
book is an *introduction,* with all the potential for success and disaster
that term entails. As we will see, there is an inherent struggle with both
literary ancestors and critical readers here that Roethke, competitive
as he was, could not ignore. His strategy in this struggle for attention
is bound up with the concept of self developed in the work. The poems
he chose to support this concept in the volume were not necessarily the
most "intense." Though intensity would come to be a value in
Roethke's work of the '40s, qualities like control, wit, and clarity are
foremost in Roethke's introductory volume, as the beginning and title
poem of the book shows.

"Open House" at first might seem to introduce a volume which
will delve deeply and unreservedly into the poet's emotional
experience:

My secrets cry aloud.
I have no need for tongue.
My heart keeps open house,
My doors are widely swung.
An epic of the eyes
My love, with no disguise.

In a review of *Open House* when it appeared in 1941, Rolfe Humphries stated that the title of the poem and the opening lines "at once give the reader to understand that much of the material to follow will be largely self-centered.... His open house is indeed wide open, from attic to basement." [2] Twenty years later Ralph J. Mills, Jr. went even further: "The poem is sharp in its personal disclosure and might justifiably serve as a motto for all of Roethke's subsequent verse." [3] "Open House" does introduce a body of work focussed largely on the self, as these two critics note, but a careful look at the poem shows that the vision of self it introduces is not nearly as "open" as it might seem.

Open House

My secrets cry aloud.
I have no need for tongue.
My heart keeps open house,
My doors are widely swung.
An epic of the eyes
My love, with no disguise.

My truths are all foreknown,
This anguish self-revealed.
I'm naked to the bone,
With nakedness my shield.
Myself is what I wear:
I keep the spirit spare.

The anger will endure,
The deed will speak the truth
In language strict and pure.
I stop the lying mouth:

Rage warps my clearest cry
To witless agony.

The poem begins with a denial of its own reason for existence: "My secrets cry aloud. / I have no need for tongue." There is a basic conflict here between the subject matter— the poet's personal secrets—and the expression of the secrets; the former is presumably so powerful that it makes the latter, and by extension the poem as a whole, superfluous. It is not verbal artifice which expresses the secrets but rather the raw emotional power of the secrets themselves; they do not have to be given "tongue" because they "cry aloud" on their own. In line 8 the poet asserts that his "anguish" is not communicated through language but is rather "self-revealed." This emphasis on personal honesty and denial of artifice is the main thrust of the first half of the poem. We learn in the first nine lines that it is the poet's emotional identity— his "heart," his "love," his "anguish," and his "truths"— which bursts into self-revelation, and the line that concludes the first half of the poem denies all artifice or "disguise": "I'm naked to the bone." Up to this point the poem does indeed seem a "motto" for Roethke's later work; in its emphasis on the direct revelation of self it appears to presage the close examination of identity in *The Lost Son* and subsequent work.

However, it is after this line, at the very center of the piece, that the poem begins to turn. Lines 9 and 10 form a paradoxical sentence: "I'm naked to the bone, / With nakedness my shield." A man with a shield is neither naked nor open. If nakedness is a shield, it protects something which is not "self-revealed." The second half of "Open House," starting with line 10, discusses this protecting shield. "Myself is what I wear"; the self, instead of being linked to openness as it is in the first half of the poem, is now metaphorically connected with clothes, a "shield" against openness. In contrast to the opening nine lines, which stress emotional self-revelation with no attempt at "disguise" or artifice, the last line of the second stanza implies an element of control: "I keep the spirit spare." As the self has changed from a kind of naked personal identity to a suit of clothes that can be put on, the "I" in the poem has changed from an agent in a process of complete emotional revelation to a controlling presence which limits and pares down the "spirit."

This emphasis on control is continued in the last stanza of the poem, where the controlling device is identified as verbal artifice. After having dismissed language as unnecessary in line 2, Roethke comes in the third stanza to stress the importance of "language strict and pure" in preserving the truth of both "deeds" and the expression of the "mouth." The motivating force behind the actions and verbal expression is emotion, which by the end of the poem is seen entirely in negative terms: "anger," "Rage," "agony." The reason these feelings are treated critically is revealed in the poem's final couplet: "Rage warps my clearest cry / To witless agony." Emotions, instead of being able to "self-reveal" themselves, bypassing the "tongue," actually "warp" clear expression. By the end of "Open House," Roethke has moved from praise of emotional openness and criticism of artifice to a sense of artifice as a weapon in a battle for clarity against the distorting power of feelings.

The concept of wit is important here. The wit of the couplet is that it states that emotions have won the battle against control while showing by its own clarity of form and statement that "rage" has *not* warped the poet's "clearest cry." It is witty to say, "I have no wit" in a witty way, just as it is witty to declare emotional "open house" with doors "widely swung" in a poem which makes only abstract references to personal feelings and contradicts the concept of openness by its lockstep meter and tight rhyme scheme. The conscious use of paradox is at the heart of the closing couplet and of "Open House" as a whole. That Roethke was aware of the paradox "Open House" presents is apparent from an earlier title he considered for the poem: "Strange Distortion" (TR 26–1). His reasons for eventually rejecting this are clear: the title would have made the paradox obvious and diminished the movement and surprise in the poem; it would have made it more direct, less witty.

I do not mean to imply that "Open House" and the other poems in the volume are mere intellectual exercises with little relation to Roethke's emotions. The poet uses control and wit as a way of communicating truths that are not "foreknown." A letter from Robert Hillyer, one of Roethke's first mentors, in 1933 stresses the work involved in attaining this communication:

> You have the gift—whatever it is—but you are sometimes self-indulgent. What you feel and think is poetry, but you do not always hammer away sufficiently at the mere artistry. Your mood is metaphysical, and that means that your expression must be correspondingly hard, simple, tough-fibred. I think you are sometimes a little

lazy in letting words— adjectives, generally— do your work for you. Why not shape these experiences into things as tangible as the pen with which you write of them?

... I believe your chief faults to be vagueness of diction and imagery and the failure to embody what you know to be true in language which all can see to be true. (TR 7–1)

Hillyer's comments, with their emphasis on "tangibility" and a "tough-fibred" poetic stance, reflect the vogue for metaphysical poetry current in the 1930s. As Louis Martz notes, Roethke was a great admirer of the taut lyrics of Louise Bogan, Elinor Wylie, and the young Stanley Kunitz, and the metaphysical mode in which these poets worked clearly influenced Roethke's own verse at the time.[4] The primary goal, as Hillyer suggests, was to make complex experience "tangible" in spare, concrete images. As he worked toward a "language strict and pure" in "Open House," Roethke decreased the "self-indulgence" of uncontrolled emotional expression. The self is linked to discipline— "I keep the spirit spare"— and is "worn" like clothes to protect against the onslaught of chaotic emotions. It is not so much revealed as created in the act of writing. Though the self is not "open," it is nonetheless authentic and honest, "naked to the bone." In perhaps the most perceptive review of *Open House*, W. H. Auden illuminates the paradox of a self which is both "naked" and a "shield":

> Both in life and art the human task is to create a necessary order out of an arbitrary chaos. A *necessary* order implies that the process of its creation is not itself arbitrary; one is not free to create *any* order one chooses. The order realized must, in fact, have been already latent in the chaos, so that successful creation is a process of discovery. [Auden's emphasis][5]

The true self is created in the work not through attempts at open revelation but through the discovery of the appropriate verbal order for dealing with personal material. As William Meredith puts it, "Poetry is obliged to set experience in order," not vice-versa.[6]

Relying as it does on artistic skill, the vision of self Roethke developed in "Open House" is effective as part of the young poet's introduction of himself in his first volume. In her introduction to a

selection of Roethke's work in the anthology *Trial Balances*, published in 1935, Louise Bogan noted three tests to differentiate good
young poets from mediocre ones:

> In the work of beginners destined to keep on writing for the rest
> of their lives, a kind of resonance is present which does not, in
> any degree, exist in the productions of those who will never put
> pen to paper after they are twenty-five. This resonance is the most
> important guide, since good poetry written at any age is primarily
> recognized by its sound. There is another test. The young *writer*
> will work, from the start, toward a clarification of emotion, that is,
> he will not fall to the ground with his subject, or try to translate
> thinly disguised life into literature, by means of decorative tricks.
> The last test is: he or she who grasps the pen will recognize it as a
> tool, and be acutely conscious of form. [Bogan's emphasis][7]

It is difficult to prove that "Open House" has "resonance," but it is
clear that the poem is the work of a young poet "acutely conscious of
form." Based as it is on formal discipline, the vision of self Roethke
presents in "Open House" and his first volume as a whole is that of a
poet who will not just express vague personal feelings but rather work
toward "a clarification of emotion" through careful artistry; his sense
of identity as something created by work rather than revealed by confession indicates that he will not merely "translate" his life into verse.
"Open House" introduces a poet opposed to self-pity. We can see how
important this is in a first volume by considering the title Roethke's
friend John Holmes proposed for the work: *Journey from Despair*
(TR 7–11).

Though Holmes' proposed title is pretentious and self-pitying, it
does reflect Roethke's personal troubles during the '30s when he was
writing the volume. These include worries about attaining and holding
teaching positions during the Depression; problems in living with his
sister and mother during the summers; anxiety in regard to his own
mental stability— Roethke suffered a breakdown in the winter of
1935–1936—and the lingering, if largely unconscious, psychological
turmoil caused by the death of his father. These troubles do not appear
directly in Roethke's volume, but the vision of self developed in *Open
House* through the title poem and, as we will see, through the selection
of poems for the volume and their arrangement in sections, represents

a kind of response to the problems at this point in Roethke's life, as well as an attempt to meet the challenge of a first volume. In his later work, particularly *The Lost Son* and *Praise to the End!*, Roethke would be able to delve more specifically into his emotional experience. In *Open House*, however, his aim was to "keep the spirit spare." He needed to create a sense of identity in the work which could prevent the "rage" he felt inside from turning his verse into "witless agony."

The vision of self *Open House* projects was not a static concept Roethke had already determined when he began the volume. It was built up over time as he worked on putting the book together. An important part of this work was Roethke's development of the five numbered sections of the finished volume. Several critics have interpreted these sections. In his review of *Open House* when it appeared in 1941, John Holmes saw the different parts this way:

> The first is personal pronoun; the second the out-of-doors; the third is premonition of darker things—death among them; the fourth is the purest of metaphysical wit, something very rare in our time; and the fifth contains still another side of the poet's nature, the human awareness of which he has become capable in his recent development.[8]

Karl Malkoff generally agrees with Holmes' sense of the sections but focusses more sharply on the self in each part. Here is what he calls the volume's "plan of organization":

  I. From analytic probing to vision as a means of knowing the self.
 II. The self seen in terms of the correspondence between inner and outer reality.
III. The self defined by nonbeing, by negation.
 IV. The self seen from the distance of comic perspective.
  V. The self in its social context.[9]

Though both Holmes and Malkoff correctly identify the subject matter and tone of Parts II, IV, and V, their ideas of those sections centered on problems of the self, Parts I and III, are less satisfactory. Part III does contain some dark poems, as Holmes notes, but these poems do not predominate in the section. Certain poems in Part III such as "Genesis" with its concept of the core of energy within the self, and "Reply

to Censure," with its confident defiance of "cravens," actually reflect a
more positive sense of identity than the largely defensive image seen
in poems like "Open House" or "The Adamant" in Part I. Malkoff's
idea that Part I affirms vision as a means of self-knowledge does not
square with the concept of identity seen in the opening poem. "Myself
is what I wear," Roethke writes, and it is this sense of identity as a
created artifice that Malkoff's interpretation misses. Malkoff sees the
whole volume as an exploration of "modes of knowing the self,"[10] but
in *Open House* Roethke was not so much investigating an identity he
already had as forging one through writing.

If we think of the organization of *Open House* in terms of how
Roethke was presenting, developing, and defending a concept of
identity before the reader, we derive something like this structure,
with some representative poems listed in parentheses:

    I. Introduction and definition of the created self ("Open House"),
       with particular reference to metaphysical issues of body and
       spirit ("Prayer," "Orders for the Day"), internal and external
       experience ("The Adamant").
    II. Interlude, in which Roethke shows us his skill at conventional
       nature poetry ("Slow Season," "The Coming of the Cold").
    III. Return to the concept of the created self and its further develop-
       ment, with both new positive aspects—the self as a growing
       unit (" 'Long Live the Weeds' "), the energy at the core ("Gen-
       esis," "Reply to Censure")—and a deeper look at personal
       chaos and dissolution ("Silence," "Against Disaster").
    IV. Second interlude, in which Roethke displays his skill at light
       verse ("For an Amorous Lady"), treats many of the earlier
       themes in the book comically ("Vernal Sentiment," "Verse
       with Allusions"), and stresses the everyday side of himself
       ("Prayer before Study," "My Dim-Wit Cousin").
    V. Analysis of contemporary society, including criticism of
       individuals and social classes ("The Favorite," "Highway:
       Michigan," "Idyll") but an affirmative view of the world as a
       whole ("Ballad of the Clairvoyant Widow," "Night Journey").

Considering *Open House* as an attempt by a young poet to persuade
the reader of the value of his work, we can see the importance of this
particular arrangement of the sections. The two interludes, Parts II and

IV, provide relief after the intense and often difficult work focussed on the self in Parts I and III. The social poems of Part V cap the book with Roethke's vision of life in general. But before the young poet can take the rather bold step of telling us about the world at the end of the volume, he needs to put his own house in order if he is to gain our trust. He must not only define himself for us but demonstrate understanding and control of both personal experience and poetic technique. Thus both Parts I and III, with their focus on the self, and the interludes, with their poetic "performances" within the standard conventions of nature poetry and light verse, help to predispose us in favor of the book's concluding section, to prove to us, in effect, that this poet is someone worth reading.

If this discussion tends to make the volume sound like an intellectual wrestling match between poet and reader, it is nonetheless an accurate reflection of Roethke's concerns in arranging the poems in *Open House*. I have already mentioned how Roethke was troubled by the rejections of his manuscript; between 1938 and 1940 it was turned down four times.[11] The angry letter to Macmillan Roethke drafted was primarily in response to the editors' criticism of his work as "poets' verse with a narrow range of appeal" (TR 9–16). This clearly struck a nerve with Roethke. His worries about being seen as a poet of limited appeal are apparent as early as 1935, when he complained that the selection of his poems in *Trial Balances*— which included no light verse, nature poetry, or poems about society—did not represent him fully (TR 15–3). The idea of thematic sections as a means to address these concerns appeared fairly late in Roethke's work on *Open House*. In a description of the manuscript he submitted for the Yale Younger Poets Prize in the spring of 1938, he noted that there were "no divisions" (TR 146–14). But by October, 1939, he had developed a sense of five different categories, listed here in the cover letter he sent with *Open House* to Henry Holt and Company:

> The book is a bit different, I think, from most volumes of verse in that it represents the Ordinary Man in several phases of modern experience: there are "nature" poems, love poems, metaphysical poems, social poems, and a whole section of light verse. (TR 16–6)

Three of the sections here—"nature" poems, social poems, and light verse—can be easily identified as Parts II, V, and IV of the published text. The other two categories, metaphysical poems and love poems, correspond loosely to Parts I and III, as we will see. However, it is important to note that though Roethke had a sense of the variety of work he was doing in 1939, he was not entirely clear about the two sections which eventually delineated the central concept of identity in *Open House*.

He was also not clear about the final order of the sections. By July of 1940 he had begun to define the third section not as love poems but as "personal" work; his sense of the sequence of parts was evolving too: "I have rearranged the book by types— nature, metaphysical, 'personal,' funny ones, the social. I have one copy the old way & one this way" (TR 147–25). The order Roethke proposes here reverses the first and second sections of the published text. It opens the volume with the largely conventional nature poems and decreases the emphasis on the creation of self in the work by "hiding" the title poem in the second section. Though the poet has come to the idea that the social vision should conclude the volume, the interludes of nature poetry and light verse are not used effectively to separate the more intense sections on the self. Roethke sent a copy of the manuscript as it was arranged in the summer of 1940 to Katherine Anne Porter and received this response:

> I wish you could change the order in one particular.... [Porter's ellipsis] I can very well be wrong, but the first part ought to be further back in the book. Let the present second part lead off.... If in case you make the change, so that the Poem called Prayer comes first, you may want to choose another to lead with. (TR 11–16)

Porter's letter not only pointed out the problem of starting the volume with the nature poems but also suggested a rearrangement of the poems within what was then Part II to increase its effectiveness as the new opening section of the book. We have already seen how the first poem of *Open House* presents the central issue in the volume and helps unify the work; this is what we might expect of a title poem, especially when it leads off a book. If "Prayer," Roethke's original choice for the opening of the section, had become the first poem in *Open House*, the focus on identity in the volume would have been muted. Roethke's decision to use his title poem as the new opening poem of the book helped define and emphasize his self-presentation in *Open House*. With this choice and the re-ordering of the five sections, Roethke developed cohesion in both the aesthetic structure of the book and its vision of identity.

The arrangement of sections was not the only means of attaining unity in *Open House*. As he completed the book, Roethke revised individual poems and removed a number of previously published poems from the collection. He describes this process in a draft of a letter to his editor at Knopf: "Here's the manuscript, scrubbed and rubbed no end. I've tried very hard to eliminate all the possibly weak, soft, or 'influenced' pieces" (TR 16–8). The terms Roethke uses here reflect the sense of self the completed *Open House* presents: one that is strong, hard, and victorious in the struggle against the influence of literary ancestors. Like the arrangement of sections, the selection of poems for the book involved more than aesthetic considerations alone. In Roethke's choices we can see the creation of self in this volume on a basic level.

In the summer of 1937 John Holmes put together a volume of Roethke's poetry to date, pasting all the manuscripts Roethke had sent him into a blank book. Though this collection does not contain all the poems Roethke had completed at that time, *Poems of Theodore Roethke* (TR 26–1), as Holmes titled it, provides a good selection of the "weak, soft, or 'influenced' pieces" Roethke excluded from *Open House*.[12] Though "weak" and "soft" can mean a variety of things when applied to a poem, "influenced" is a fairly clear term. In his essay "How to Write Like Somebody Else" Roethke notes two imitative poems he eliminated from *Open House*: "The Buds Now Stretch," borrowed from the work of Leonie Adams; and "This Light," with obvious echoes of Elinor Wylie, Shelley, and Vaughn (SP 63–66). Roethke had found both these works good enough for publication in periodicals, in 1938 and 1934, respectively,[13] but when they were considered as part of his first volume they appeared too "influenced." Nevertheless, literary ancestors are present in *Open House*, as " 'Long Live the Weeds,' " with its acknowledged derivation from Hopkins, shows. The difference between effective and ineffective relations to literary models becomes clear when we compare this poem with "Praise," another work based on Hopkins which was excluded from *Open House*:

"Long Live the Weeds"
Hopkins

Long live the weeds that overwhelm
My narrow vegetable realm!
The bitter rock, the barren soil
That force the son of man to toil;
All things unholy, marred by curse,
The ugly of the universe.
The rough, the wicked, and the wild
That keep the spirit undefiled.
With these I match my little wit
And earn the right to stand or sit,
Hope, love, create, or drink and die:
These shape the creature that is I.

Praise

A praise to the resilient: to bones in barred wings
That hold hawks motionless in rushing air;
The salt-encrusted sail that survives without tear;
Up-springing weed marking the unwary with stings;
Whip-handle and hoe; needles; plucked guitar strings;

Cunning with compromise: the devious turning and
          twisting when Armenian meets voluble Greek;
Disingenuous tongue in the turned other cheek;
The boxer's feint with flickering left fist;
And, though fretted and frayed, the nerves, the
          will to resist.[14]

Though " 'Long Live the Weeds,' " as Jenijoy La Belle points out,
derives from a line in Hopkins' "Inversnaid"[15] and develops a theme of
acceptance of the struggle with chaotic elements which is similar to
one seen in Hopkins' work, it does not *sound* like a Hopkins poem.
"Praise," on the other hand, makes use of a kind of sprung rhythm,
heavy alliteration, and descriptive compression through inversion and
participial adjectives— "Up-springing weed," "the turned other

cheek"—all trademarks of Hopkins' style. In its title and diction—the general statement followed by a long series of images with no full stops—it is clearly imitative of Hopkins' "Pied Beauty": "He fathers-forth whose beauty is past change: / Praise Him."[16]

Referring to this poem in a letter, Roethke noted the difference between "assimilation" and "imitation" which is the key here (SL 81–82). "Praise," as the poet eventually discovered, imitates the poetic ancestor in style, rhetoric, and concept; it depends for its power as a poem on the stylistic and thematic work done by Hopkins. In " 'Long Live the Weeds,' " on the other hand, we see a poet writing in his own style in response to Hopkins' line; the poem is notable not for its skill in repeating a Hopkins "performance" but for Roethke's unique understanding and development of Hopkins' basic point. The assimilation of Hopkins here involves the young poet absorbing an influence and dealing with it in his own way. The assimilator is in control of the material he assimilates. Imitation is essentially the reverse; the young poet's identity is hidden by the style and ideas of his predecessor. Though Roethke later described conscious imitation as "one of the great methods, perhaps *the* method of learning to write" (SP 69, Roethke's emphasis), he could not afford to present himself as a neophyte in his first volume. To include imitative poems like "Praise" or "This Light" in *Open House* would undercut his definition of self in the work; it would be an admission that he did not have strict enough control of his own identity as a poet to fend off the influences of others.

As La Belle notes, Roethke took the struggle with literary ancestors quite seriously in his first volume.[17] The poem "Feud," for example, invokes "The menace of ancestral eyes" and concludes with this warning to descendants:

> This ancient feud
> Is seldom won. The spirit starves
> Until the dead have been subdued.

The "dead" are not only literary forefathers but also literal ones here. Roethke's tendency to conflate real and figurative ancestors, seen most clearly in his habit of calling mentors like Kenneth Burke "Pa," comes out in the two levels of reference in "Feud" and other early poems and suggests that the young poet's struggle to assert his own identity as a writer is parallel to his struggle against parental influences, particularly those of his father, in growing up. The death of

Roethke's father while the poet was still a teenager left unresolved tensions, and Roethke's sense of the literary choice between the destruction of identity in mere imitation of ancestors and the development of an independent self through assimilation has parallels in the struggle between father and son. Though Roethke would not be able to develop the psychological ramifications of this conflict until the aesthetic and personal breakthrough of his second book, there are several references to this issue in *Open House*, including mention of a "father's ghost" spoiling the son's honeymoon in "Prognosis" and protagonists haunted by ancestors in "Orders for the Day," "My Dim-Wit Cousin," and "Sale." "Subduing the dead" is primarily a literary task in *Open House*, but the psychological dimension will become increasingly important later in Roethke's career.

"Weak" is the most general of the three critical terms Roethke applied to the poems excluded from *Open House*. On one level the term refers to works that were just not up to Roethke's poetic standards when he was putting the volume together. In this category are several poems that deal with topics seen in *Open House* but treat them in a "weaker" fashion than do the poems in the completed text. Here, for example, is a poem which echoes the included poems "No Bird" and "Death Piece" in both subject and form:

There Is No Word

There is no word that can be said
In this imperial peace.
The quiet wrapped about his head
Bespeaks the mind's surcease.

His shadow is dispersed, its size
Is lost in rolling shade.
Withhold the anguishment of eyes
For tongueless accolade.

It is easy to see why Roethke rejected this poem and kept the other two. The two stanzas of "There Is No Word" lack the evocative images of the other two poems, the hive "sealed honey-tight" in "Death Piece" and the still "forest of the dead" in "No Bird." The excluded poem also displays the weaknesses of awkward vocabulary—"anguishment," "Bespeaks"—and straining for rhyme in the "peace"-"surcease" link of the first stanza and the use of "size"—How can a "size" be "lost"?—purely to rhyme with "eyes" in the second stanza. Roethke also eliminated several weaker pieces on the important theme of the conflict between body and spirit in the finished text. The closing stanzas of the excluded "Prepare Thyself" show a simple-mindedness on both the stylistic and thematic levels:

> Fleshly machine of lust
> Is deftly thrust
> Beneath the level dust.
>
> But soul, intrepid, white,
> And blind with light,
> Leaps to the Infinite!

Two others in this vein, "Second Version" and "The Knowing Heart," were rejected after Louise Bogan found them confusing and "slight," respectively (TR 3–15). Descriptive poems such as "Summer Night" and "Evening Prelude" were eliminated apparently for not being as vivid and evocative as "The Light Comes Brighter" or the other nature poems in Part II of the published text.

In the process of choosing work for the different sections of the volume, some categories were eliminated entirely. For example, there are no serious love poems in *Open House*, though pieces like "Now We the Two" and "Sonnet" among the excluded work in *Poems of Theodore Roethke* show the poet was writing them; as we have seen, he originally considered including a whole section of them (TR 16–6). As Roethke developed the concept of self that *Open House* projects, works which describe intimate personal contact with another had to be eliminated. Love poems would be too "soft" for the general tone of *Open House*, as would another type of poem Roethke was writing during the '30s: the poem of vision and transcendence. Like several other works in *Poems of Theodore Roethke*, "Some Day I'll Step" describes a release from earthly existence into "a brighter realm of space." Here the poet concludes:

> Death shall not drift my limbs apart
> When ancient silence storms my heart:

Before my patterned dance is done,
I'll pace on shadows to the sun.

How delicate will motion be
In this, my fleet identity!

The easy escape from the real world through imaginative vision here would run counter to the stress on the self facing conflict squarely in poems in the finished volume like "Reply to Censure" and " 'Long Live the Weeds.' " In like manner Roethke eliminated "We Sighed for a Sign" with its benign but clearly unearned vision at the end:

New landmarks will emerge after glacial scourge
A triumphal richness will well from the heart's core
New faith will unfold the truth burgeon forth.

The scarcity of punctuation emphasizes the non-rational, transcendent nature of the poet's vision here, one which he found too unrealistic and too facile for *Open House*.

Other "soft" poems—and here "soft" and "weak" become synonymous—display the self not as dreamy and visionary but as pathetic and helpless. In *Theodore Roethke: The Garden Master* Rosemary Sullivan notes the poet's early attempt to reveal the source of his psychic troubles in "Difficult Grief."[18] However, as we have seen, *Open House* is based not on self-revelation but self-creation, and the conclusion of this rejected poem was both too self-revealing and too self-pitying for the volume:

And though it leave it will return
To mock me with a bitterer scorn:
Old desolation, young dismay,
A sorrow ponderable as clay,
A fear too shameful to confess,
A terrible child-loneliness.

The two poems about his mental breakdown Roethke published in 1937, "Meditation in Hydrotherapy" and "Lines upon Leaving a Sanitarium,"[19] are excluded for obvious reasons; in addition to rebuking the sense of control over self *Open House* develops, the latter poem throws into question the whole issue of even attempting to define one's identity: "Self-contemplation is a curse / That makes an old confusion worse." In "Immediacy" Roethke describes himself as "a being cursed with sight," extending the attack beyond self-analysis to perception itself. Though some poems included in *Open House* involve a similar critical approach to the self, even the darker poems in the volume like "Silence" or "Against Disaster" do not assert that perceiving reality is worthless; this would undercut the entire volume, which, after all, is made up of Roethke's perceptions.

If the self in poems like "Immediacy" and "Difficult Grief" is pathetic and unable to control the emotional and sensory experience that overwhelms it, the self in another group of excluded poems is pompous and phony. "My Proper Self Goes Out" is a good example:

My Proper Self Goes Out

My former self goes out;
The flesh is purified.
The past will be my foil
Against ridiculous doubt.
Discord shall not prevail
While blood beats in my side.

The body learned its length
And breadth; my darkest mood
Was written with my name.
Now I declare my strength
And find a proper theme:
My vigor is renewed.

I drop my foolish ways
For wisdom dearly bought,
And salvage what I can
Out of my wasted days.
The present is my span:
I move to richer thought.

Roethke is working here with the three-stress line used often in *Open House*, and the three stanzas of "My Proper Self Goes Out" develop a concept of identity similar to that in the title poem. However, it is not convincing for the poet merely to "declare" his "strength"; there must be some conflict within the poem to show that the strength is there. The problem with "My Proper Self Goes Out" is that it is, as a later title indicates, just a "Statement" (SL 57–58). Not only is the poet's claim of strength untested in the poem, but the language itself sounds vague and pretentious: "ridiculous doubt," "my wasted days," "wisdom dearly bought." Another poem in this vein, "The Only Destiny," ends with the same fierce but hollow vision of self: "Concentric mind, direct the only / Destiny, the fierce and lonely." There is a romantic tone to the poet's supplication here; the vision of self is made glamorous in its "fierce" loneliness. "Didactic," the title Roethke eventually gave the poem,[20] shows his final understanding that the sense of self was not created through the poem but rather just stated. In his comments on "The Conqueror," another poem of this type, Blessing compares the awkward "heightening" of the poet's voice to that of "a lecturer's when facing an audience he wishes to impress."[21] In poems like "Didactic" and "Statement" we receive a rhetorically inflated "lecture" on the strength of the poet's sense of identity instead of a convincing demonstration of that strength in conflict.

A pompous self, a pathetic self, an individual identity distorted by the influence of poetic ancestors—these and other visions of self were excluded as Roethke removed the "weak, soft, or 'influenced' pieces" from *Open House*. But the poet also excluded some work that did not fit these categories. A letter to Stanley Kunitz (SL 53–56) shows that Roethke had a draft of the poem "River Incident" as early as 1937. The fact that this poem was not included in *Open House* but published seven years later in Roethke's second volume, *The Lost Son and Other Poems*, indicates that the poet was not merely including all of his good poems to date in his first book. Though his sense of the second volume was rudimentary in 1937, Roethke did have an idea of the limitations of the first. "River Incident" concludes with a sense of primeval *déjà vu*, emphasizing a deep organic union between the poet and the ooze in which life began:

And I knew I had been there before,
In that cold, granitic slime,
In the dark, in the rolling water.

The vision of self here is allied with that in the greenhouse poems of Roethke's second volume; it is much more fluid and less controlled than that in *Open House*.

It is partially this element of fluidity that leads me to call two poems included in *Open House* precursors of the work in Roethke's second volume. "The Premonition" echoes the draft of "River Incident" in its loose and varied three-stress rhythm—quite different from that in "Open House" or other trimeter poems in the volume—its lack of stanzaic breaks, and its irregular rhyme scheme based largely on slant and feminine rhymes:

The Premonition

Walking this field I remember
Days of another summer.
Oh that was long ago! I kept
Close to the heels of my father,
Matching his stride with half-steps
Until we came to a river.
He dipped his hand in the shallow:
Water ran over and under
Hair on a narrow wrist bone;
His image kept following after,—
Flashed with the sun in the ripple.
But when he stood up, that face
Was lost in a maze of water.

"On the Road to Woodlawn" has a stricter rhyme scheme, but the long lines in its two stanzas are rhythmically looser than those in most poems of *Open House*:

On the Road to Woodlawn

I miss the polished brass, the powerful black horses,
The drivers creaking the seats of the baroque hearses,
The high-piled floral offerings with sentimental verses,
The carriages reeking with varnish and stale perfume.

I miss the pallbearers momentously taking their places,

> The undertaker's obsequious grimaces,
> The craned necks, the mourners' anonymous faces,
> —And the eyes, still vivid, looking up from a sunken room.

Stylistic fluidity alone does not make these two poems precursors of the later work; there is also the overall relation of the self to experience. Discussing "The Premonition," Louis Martz notes several aspects of this new relation which apply to "On the Road to Woodlawn" as well, including the poet's reliance on "implication" and "mystery" instead of logical development, his "open display of feeling," and his cultivation of memory.[22] As personal memories, these two poems contain specific references to the poet's father, seen nowhere else in *Open House*. Woodlawn is the cemetery where Roethke's extended confrontation with his father's death in the later "Lost Son" sequence begins; the "premonition" in the title of the other poem also refers to the father's death, as the last two lines indicate. In the numinous, almost supernatural scenes these poems describe, the father's presence in memory and Roethke's deep sense of loss predominate. The self is more specific and more vulnerable in these two poems than anywhere else in *Open House*. Roethke's inclusion of them in the published text suggests that by 1941 he was not yet aware of the father-son theme as a basic part of *The Lost Son* in the way he was aware of the "organic" theme seen in "River Incident." The poems in his second book which really examine the father-son relation, the "Lost Son" sequence in Part IV, were not composed until the mid-'40s. In the next chapter we will see how changes in the poet's writing methods in "On the Road to Woodlawn" and the later greenhouse work helped Roethke delve more deeply into his own past in *The Lost Son*.

While the composition of a significant part of the second volume involved Roethke's working through a series of poems to find out essentially who he was—a method the poet later described as "cyclic" (SP 39)—*Open House* is based, as we have seen, on the careful selection and arrangement of individual poems. A sense of identity is not so much revealed to the poet through his work on the book as it is created by the artifice itself. If we look at *Open House* in the light of Auden's idea that a good poet "can be recognized by his tense awareness of both chaos and order,"[23] Roethke's first volume clearly tends more toward order than chaos. But the element of conscious artifice and control in *Open House* is, as Auden points out, "a *necessary* order." Without it the poet's sense of self would have dissolved in "witless agony." Before Roethke could undertake the deeper self-exploration of *The Lost Son*, he had to create and defend an identity as man and poet in his first volume. It was necessary for Roethke to prove that the core of self existed before he could examine what lay hidden within it.

CHAPTER THREE

From *Open House* to the Greenhouse:
Roethke's Poetic Breakthrough

> My first book was much too wary, much too gingerly in its
> approach to experience; rather dry in tone and constricted in
> rhythm. I am trying to loosen up, to write poems of greater intensity
> and symbolical depth. (SL 114)

By the mid-1940s, Theodore Roethke had become aware of the
limitations of his first volume and had immersed himself in new work
of a significantly different order. The seven-year period between the
publication of *Open House* in 1941 and *The Lost Son and Other Poems*
in 1948 is considered pivotal by many critics. Ralph J. Mills, Jr. refers
to the "imaginative leap" Roethke made during this time[1] and Stephen
Spender describes the poet's work after this "leap" as that which is
"most uniquely Roethke."[2] Kenneth Burke sees the period in which
Roethke was working on his second volume as one centered on the
poet's "most important breakthrough," citing Roethke's greenhouse
poems in Part I of *The Lost Son* as the embodiment of the change.[3] As
Burke and others note, this breakthrough was not only stylistic but
also psychological. Characterized by the development of what Mills
calls an "intensely subjective vision,"[4] Roethke's less "wary"
"approach to experience" after the breakthrough reflected a new relation between his writing and his sense of self. We have already seen
how Roethke essentially created a sense of identity through his selection and arrangement of poems for *Open House*. In this chapter I want
to look more closely at the actual process of writing—including notebook work, drafts, and revisions—in order to illuminate Roethke's
development between *Open House* and the next volume. My focus
will be primarily on the composition of three poems: "Genesis," a representative example of Roethke's work from the mid-1930s; the transitional poem "On the Road to Woodlawn" from the late '30s; and

"Cuttings," the opening piece in the greenhouse sequence, dating from the mid-'40s. Examining Roethke's work on these poems in his notebooks and drafts, we can see changes in both the way he wrote and the way he felt about what he wrote which are the underpinnings of the poet's extraordinary breakthrough.

Here is the final text of "Genesis" as it appeared in *Open House:*

Genesis

This elemental force
Was wrested from the sun;
A river's leaping source
Is locked in narrow bone.

This wisdom floods the mind,
Invades quiescent blood;
A seed that swells the rind
To burst the fruit of good.

A pearl within the brain,
Secretion of the sense;
Around a central grain
New meaning grows immense.

This poem was first published in *The Nation* in 1936 and is typical of much of Roethke's early work. The end-stopped, metrical lines—there are no rhythmic substitutions—and the tight rhyme scheme give the feeling of fierce energy controlled by form. The central image of the poem, the "pearl within the brain," parallels that of two other *Open House* poems in iambic trimeter quatrains, "The Adamant" and "Reply to Censure." Based on a dichotomy between self and world which is announced in the title poem of *Open House*, "Genesis," like the other two poems, develops the concept of an inviolable core of personal identity.[5] "Open House," as we have seen, calls for "language strict and pure" which will "keep the spirit spare." Relying heavily on direct statements, unelaborated images, and abstractions, the language of "Genesis" meets this definition. As "Open House" indicates, the tightly controlled style derived from such "pure" language and strict adherence to the demands of rhyme and meter is a way of keeping the spirit "spare," constraining the self within the bounds of the conscious will. The style of "Genesis," in keeping with the central thrust of Roethke's first volume, reflects not only the poet's interest in the taut, metaphysical lyric but also his sense of the self as an entity to be controlled and ordered through the process of writing.

The composition of poetry, however, is not entirely a function of the conscious will. As Auden noted in his review of *Open House*, writing involves finding the "necessary order" latent in chaotic experience, "so that successful creation is a process of discovery."[6] The finished text, embodying this order, stresses conscious control over experience, but in order to determine the inherent order Roethke had to decrease his control somewhat, to make himself more open to different possibilities in the initial stages of writing. The origins of "Genesis" in the poet's notebooks reveal this partial suspension of will as Roethke works toward his first sense of the poem. Roethke's use of rhyme and meter in this preliminary work is an example. In the completed text of "Genesis," these formal aspects emphasize the poet's conscious, rational control over his material. However, in the primary stage of composition, Roethke's use of rhyme and a repeating rhythm shows his reliance on the sounds of words, not their meanings, as a way of generating poetic material. The notebook in which the first work on "Genesis" was done contains a number of disconnected lines and couplets—such as "A haze before the sun," "Arise from red-eyed ache," and "Its attributes are worn" (TR 33–20)—before Roethke puts together a recognizable stanza. These fragments are not unified by a particular concept, an idea the poet has consciously chosen to develop, but rather by their common iambic trimeter rhythm. Order exists only at the primitive level of repetition in rhythm. At this early stage of composition, then, Roethke is using meter as a device to generate lines without a clear sense of what he wants to say; conscious acts of arrangement, clarification, and judgment are held in abeyance.

Rhyme is employed in a similar manner:

What splits its way through rock
Like subterranean fire

The creeping flame, desire,
Will seek its way through rock

A ravenous tongue of flame

Remote in deepest shock.

(TR 33–20)

"Fire" leads the poet to "desire," and "rock" leads to "shock." But what differentiates Roethke's work with these three couplets from his work with the other fragments is that links of sound are used along with conscious considerations of image and meaning as Roethke develops the hackneyed metaphor of love as flame. His sense of the inherent order in the poem has developed beyond the aural level. It is significant that, despite the clichés inherent in them, Roethke selects these three couplets from a mass of less rational but more imaginative material. Rejecting intriguing phrases like "The muscles of the wind" and "Colours scrape the eye," the poet settles on the lines most clearly molded by the conscious mind as the primary material for the conclusion of this early version of "Genesis":

> This elemental force
> Was wrested from the sun;
> A river's leaping source
> Is locked in narrow bone.

> This love is lusty mirth
> That shakes eternal sky,
> The agony of birth,
> The fiercest will to die.

> The fever-heat of mind
> Within prehensile brute;
> A seed that swells the rind
> Of strange, impalpable fruit.

> This faith surviving shock,
> This smoldering desire,
> Will split its way through rock
> Like subterranean fire.

(TR 20–5)[7]

The stanzaic form of "Genesis" arises early in the process of composition. The fragmentary lines and couplets in Roethke's notebook
are followed immediately by attempts to construct an *abab* quatrain.
This early movement from fragments to the development of a stanza
reflects Roethke's interest in working with consciously crafted,
ordered material as soon in the writing process as possible. The stanza
we see emerging, however, is not the one we might expect from the
poet's attention to the "rock"-"shock" couplets but rather one for
which there is no preliminary material in the notebook passage, the
second quatrain in the draft cited above. In his three attempts to complete this stanza, Roethke struggles to develop a single formal unit
before he considers the implications in what he has previously written.
His interest is clearly not so much in content, in developing a complete
thought from the preliminary material, as it is in form. Looking back
at this early notebook passage as a whole, we see that the fragmentary
material before the quatrain—though it has no relation to the stanza's
ideas or images—is nonetheless essential to the creation of the stanza
because it provides a framework of rhythm and rhyme in which the
poet can undertake more extensive work. Before this formal structure
is established, the most developed units in the notebook passage are
only a few lines long; after it, we find a group of some twenty lines on
the same topic. The earliest work in the notebook, then, can be considered a kind of poetic "gearing up," in which the repetition of the basic
trimeter rhythm and the alternate rhyming in the couplets are more
important than the meanings of individual lines and images.

Once form has been established, however, the writing process
changes. For one thing, deletions become much more frequent.
Among the forty lines and fragments of preliminary material in the
notebook passage, the poet has crossed out only two completely—
both of these in his work on the quatrain—and made small deletions of
single words or phrases in about a dozen more. At a later stage of composition, when Roethke has the first three stanzas of the draft version
done and is working on the fourth (TR 32–3), only two complete lines
out of ten are left untouched, and one-third of the lines are deleted
completely. The poet's more critical attitude toward what he has written reflects his movement from the generation of poetic material—
which involves, as we have seen, the partial suspension of the conscious will—to the transformation of the generated material into the
artifice of the poem, a process which, at this stage of Roethke's career,

is based on conscious choice. In keeping with this change, Roethke no longer uses meter and rhyme as a way of developing new images and connections but rather employs them to gain control over his material by eliminating the parts that do not fit. For example, from the preliminary couplet "A ravenous tongue of flame / Remote in deepest shock" Roethke keeps the last line for consideration but not the first; other fragments ending in " flame" or " flames" are also deleted because they do not fit the "fire"-"desire," "rock"-"shock" rhyme scheme. Rhythmic irregularities too are removed, as in the deletion of "hot" from "This ant-like flame, hot desire." Roethke even includes a list of rhymes for "shock" on the right hand side of the page, setting up a tight structure which new alternate lines must fit. These techniques help Roethke develop the "language strict and pure" "Open House" demands.

In forming and polishing individual quatrains at this stage of composition, Roethke does not concern himself much with the order of stanzas in the work. As I have mentioned, he begins with the second stanza; some pages later in the same notebook (TR 3 3–20) is a draft of the first. The first complete draft of the poem contains two stanzas which do not appear in the published text and lacks the vital concluding stanza which makes "Genesis" what it is:

> A pearl within the brain,
> Secretion of the sense;
> Around a central grain
> New meaning grows immense.

In the first two stages of composition we have seen how Roethke generates poetic material and then forms and polishes stanzaic "pearls" from it. The poet's large-scale revisions of the first complete draft mark a third stage, in which the "New meaning" of the work is developed.

In his essay "Verse in Rehearsal" Roethke quotes the comments of his friend Rolfe Humphries on the early, four-stanza version of "Genesis." Humphries' remarks, though extensive, say little about the overall meaning of the work, concentrating instead on problems like the draft's "conventional rhymes," its "monogamous adjective-noun combinations," and the redundance of the phrase "strange, impalpable fruit" in the third stanza (SP 3 3). Roethke must have considered these comments important, since he reprinted them in the essay; but the relation between Humphries' remarks and Roethke's revisions is not as direct as the essay might imply. The poet deals with most of the problems his friend notes, but instead of doing the technical "tinkering" that Humphries advises— finding a title to account for the standard rhymes; changing "strange, impalpable" to a four-syllable word— Roethke replaces everything in the poem except the opening stanza and one line in the third quatrain. One reason for this radical revision is that the poet had already done the kind of poetic polishing his friend suggests when he was working on the individual stanzas. Roethke's early sense that the draft was at least technically proficient is reflected in the fact that he submitted it to three periodicals before sending it to Humphries (TR 20–5).[8]

Roethke may have felt growing reservations about the craftsmanship of the piece as the rejection slips came in, but I think the main problems that bothered him at this final stage of the writing process had to do with the overall meaning, tone, and stance of the poem. He expresses this dissatisfaction in his comments on the draft sent to Humphries: "Sophomoric straining? Just old tricks? Or fair traditional piece?" (TR 20–5). The last of these three remarks is, of course, wishful thinking. The second comment views the "traditional" aspects of the piece from a darker perspective. In this sense the remark could be taken primarily as a sign of doubts about the conventionality of the poem's technique, as Humphries appears to read it; but it also connects with Roethke's first comment. "Sophomoric straining?" shows the poet's worries about how he appears in the poem, about whether he seems immature or phony in it. I think Roethke is referring to a pose of disembodied wisdom here, one which he has assumed before in "Prepare Thyself"—"Prepare thyself for change, / The ever-strange, / Thy soul's immortal range"— "The Knowing Heart"— "O this mortality will break / The false dissembling brain apart" (TR 26–1)[9]—and other poems he excluded from *Open House*. This kind of poetic stance—in which the poet assumes a pompous, all-knowing attitude in order to claim broad metaphysical knowledge he has not earned in the poem or in his experience—must have seemed like an "old trick" to Roethke; it is an easy way for a young poet to take on large topics. It pervades the three stanzas the poet omitted from the final draft, with their references to "prehensile brute" and "eternal sky" and their confident statements about the results of "love" and "faith surviving shock."

It might be argued that the final version of "Genesis" is also pompous in tone, with its description of "wisdom flooding the mind" and the concluding image of the "pearl within the brain." But the published text is not "sophomoric straining"; we accept its claims partially because they are toned down and made more specific than those in the earlier draft but also, and more importantly, because we can see their relation to the poet who makes them. The final text clearly traces the movement of the "elemental force" of external energy inward to the individual mind and body and its development there into the substance of the growing "pearl." The title "Genesis," which appears only after Roethke has begun work on the three-stanza version (TR 32–5), clarifies this movement by focussing our attention on the poem as a description of a creative process, with the implication that the poem itself is the result of such a process. The earlier four-stanza draft—though it has elements of the basic external-internal, energy-matter dichotomies—includes neither this progression toward the individual self nor the implied reference to the poet in the process of writing. Its tone seems impersonal and lofty, its claims unjustified by experience. In revising the poem after this draft has been completed, Roethke finds a new meaning in the work, as well as a new poetic stance, one which engages the self more effectively. The self in *Open House* is, of course, an entity created in the act of writing. Thus it is not surprising that the version of "Genesis" which presents the self most accurately and with the least pomposity is also the best in terms of Roethke's aesthetic in the volume, with a clear structure, language which has been made "strict and pure" by the deletion of confusing or unnecessary adjectives, total metrical regularity, and a rhyme scheme that is both tight and original.

"The great danger is *softness*," Roethke wrote in a letter in 1935 (TR 150–14, Roethke's emphasis). What we find in "Genesis" and other early poems is a pose which counteracts this danger by projecting a spare and inviolable core of identity: a pearl; an adamant; even, as in "Open House," a shield. This is the poetry of what Dennis E. Brown terms "the entrenched self,"[10] and behind the trenches we see few specifics of Roethke's individual identity. By the late 1930s, however, Roethke was becoming aware of the limitations of this kind of writing. In a review of Ben Belitt's *The Five-Fold Mesh* in 1939, Roethke raised some critical points which could apply to his own early work:

Often instead of being truly passionate, he is merely literary; he shapes ingenious verbal patterns, but they are not always poetry. Too much of his work seems to spring from an act of the will rather than from an inner compulsion. Except for half a dozen poems—and that is enough—he creates no more than remarkable artifice. (SP 115)

As Richard Blessing notes, Roethke began to feel dissatisfied with the "well-made poem" in the late '30s.[11] In seeking to develop his own work beyond mere "remarkable artifice," Roethke produced two intriguing poems in this period which found their way into *Open House*. As we have seen, both "The Premonition," with its reliance on unstressed line endings and half-rhyme, and "On the Road to Woodlawn," with its rough hexameter rhythm, are formally looser than the other work in *Open House*; both poems too arise from an "inner compulsion" which eventually becomes central in Roethke's work: the poet's drive to understand and communicate with his dead father. Precursors of Roethke's work in *The Lost Son*, these poems show significant differences in compositional method from that of the early work, as an analysis of the writing of "On the Road to Woodlawn" reveals.

The composition of "On the Road to Woodlawn" represents a transitional phase between Roethke's work on poems like "Genesis" in the mid-'30s and his work on the greenhouse poems in the early '40s. Here is the final text as it appeared in *Open House*:

On the Road to Woodlawn

I miss the polished brass, the powerful black horses,
The drivers creaking the seats of the baroque hearses,
The high-piled floral offerings with sentimental verses,
The carriages reeking with varnish and stale perfume.

I miss the pallbearers momentously taking their places,
The undertaker's obsequious grimaces,
The craned necks, the mourners' anonymous faces,
—And the eyes, still vivid, looking up from a sunken room.

As we might gather from the length and rhythmic variation of the lines, Roethke does not use a repeating rhythm as a way of generating material for this poem. Rather the poem has its origins in questions which lead to a gathering of imagery:

> Where is the polished brass
> ~~Where are the~~
> Or the streamlined fenders the black flags
> The line, snipped by the traffic light,
>
> (TR 33–19)

These questions reflect the process of memory which is at the heart of Roethke's work on this and many subsequent poems. While this conscious attempt to tap his own past experience through memory is a technique not seen in the preliminary work on "Genesis," we do find the same use of rhyme as a generating tool in both poems:

> I miss the powerful black horses:
> The drivers in the creaking seats of the baroque hearses;
> The high piled Floral Offerings with sentimental verses,
>
> (TR 33–19)

After this rhymed section, the poet returns in his notebook to unrhymed fragments as he works to clarify details in his memory of the funeral procession. Here, in contrast to "Genesis," the scene of the poem, existing as it does in the past, is determined considerably before the meter. On the next page of the notebook, in fact, Roethke's examination of the scene has led him from the funeral procession to his dead father, whom he now addresses in trimeter: "Far and away above you / The hissing Planets whirl." After these lines is a question in prose which concludes the work on this poem in the notebook. When Roethke asks himself, "Do the clues to our generation lie in the diseased?"—a question I take to refer to his father's slow death from cancer—he is thinking about neither the poem's form nor its descriptive detail. The question, unlike anything in the notebook work on "Genesis," reflects Roethke's concern with the meaning of the experience before the poem is written.

The issue of the personal significance of the experience for Roethke is held largely in abeyance as the poet works on completing and polishing a draft of the poem. It is in this second stage of composition that the work on this poem most closely resembles that on "Genesis." The *aaab cccb* rhyme scheme is established, and the poet tries

out different versions of lines to fit it. There is also some rhythmic tinkering, though considerably less than with "Genesis" because of the
later poem's looser metrical form. The basic work on the first stanza of
"On the Road to Woodlawn" is completed at this stage, but the second
stanza at this point is considerably different from the published text:

> Now, as if performing a task that disgraces,
> The black-flagged cars, filled with anonymous faces,
> Hurry to where, among urns, a vacant place is,
> —As if that cemetery had insufficient room.
>
> (TR 2–33)[12]

If Roethke had decided to retain this draft stanza as the conclusion of
"On the Road to Woodlawn," he would have produced a poem not
unlike "Highway: Michigan," "Idyll," or the other poems on social
topics in *Open House*, a piece beginning with observation and description from the poet's own viewpoint and including at the end a vision of
the social problem—highway mania, suburban anxiety, our inability
to deal with death—expressed in a largely impersonal way. But the
question of the personal meaning of the scene begins to concern
Roethke again after he has completed this draft; beneath the two typed
stanzas on the draft sheet is new work in pencil on what will become
the second stanza of the published text.

The most noticeable changes between the draft and published
texts of the second stanza are the clear presence of the poet himself in
the final version, signalled by the "I miss" which now repeats the
directly personal opening of the piece; and the replacement of an
objective, thematically centered last line with one based on a haunting
personal image. This concluding hallucinatory vision of the father
staring up from the casket does not resolve the movement of the poem
the way the pearl image does in "Genesis"; it does not unify the pattern
of images in the work or clarify the overall meaning of the poem. The
tight metaphysical conceit which would give "tangibility" to the experience is no longer the poet's goal. In rejecting this metaphysical
mode, Roethke gives up a measure of control over experience in favor
of a new vision of self in the work. In "On the Road to Woodlawn" the
self is presented as vulnerable, and the experience is seen as essentially irresolvable. In revising this poem in the last stage of the writing
process, Roethke does not work toward creating an identity as he had

earlier, but rather toward describing personal experience specifically and honestly.

Based as it is on memory, the composition of "On the Road to Woodlawn" involves more conscious work with the subject matter, particularly in the early stages, than does the writing of "Genesis." Paradoxically, however, "Genesis" in its final version seems a more deliberately crafted poem than "On the Road to Woodlawn." The personal stance developed in the earlier poem emphasizes the conscious awareness of "meaning" in experience, in contrast to the depiction in the later work of an emotional event the poet does not completely comprehend. Roethke's sense of the difference between these two modes of dealing with experience in poetry, as well as his increasing frustration with the "Genesis" mode, is summarized in this notebook entry: "I can suck something dry from experience, but I can't see it imaginatively" (TR 33–20).

The poet's progress toward a kind of writing which would allow him to "see experience imaginatively" was not simple or direct. For example, "The Cycle," a poem written a few years after "On the Road to Woodlawn" and included with "River Incident" and other poems on the "organic" theme in Part III of *The Lost Son,* more closely resembles "Genesis" in the way it was composed than it does the funeral poem:

The Cycle

Dark water, underground,
Beneath the rock and clay,
Beneath the roots of trees,
Moved into common day,
Rose from a mossy mound
In mist that sun could seize.

The fine rain coiled in a cloud
Turned by revolving air
Far from that colder source
Where elements cohere
Dense in the central stone.
The air grew loose and loud.

> Then, with diminished force,
> The full rain fell straight down,
> Tunneled with lapsing sound
> Under even the rock-shut ground,
> Under a river's source,
> Under primeval stone.

The trimeter rhythm is somewhat looser in "The Cycle" than in "Genesis," and there is a clearer focus on a single image pattern— these developments may be the result of Roethke's dissatisfaction with what he called the "grunt and groan rhythm" and "metaphorical rock-jumping" of "Genesis" (SP 34). However, in both poems Roethke uses sound to generate material in the notebooks (TR 33–26); develops individual stanzas without a definite sense or order, employing lists of rhyme words to polish the form (TR 18–61); and restructures the poem after the work on each stanza is practically done, adding, in both cases, a new opening stanza (TR 18–61).

Roethke's early writing methods seem to work well for a relatively impersonal poem like "The Cycle," but when the poet attempts to examine his own past with them, the result is quite different, as in this early notebook work on the greenhouse poem "Old Florist":

> I cannot claim those acres,
> The benches knocked to stone,
> The hot beds smashed to kindling
> The rose house tumbled down.
>
> Those tall hard-fingered florists
> Swearers and drinkers, they
>
> The garish shanties creep across
> The fields once full of flowers

> (TR 34–38)

These lines are essentially a false start; after them come the fragments like "spitting tobacco juice" which are the actual raw material for the poem. The problems in the lines are related, I think, to Roethke's use of meter and, in the first quatrain, rhyme. In meeting these formal demands, Roethke assumes an odd melodramatic tone, in which the self is cast in a traditional elegiac role and the subject is glamorized. Diction suffers too, as in the inverted "Swearers and drinkers, they"; in another attempt to work on this material in meter Roethke even uses the contraction "shan't" (TR 34–38). Formal techniques, then, instead of generating authentic poetic material from memory, essentially replace careful examination of past experience with language and images based on a conventional pose. In an early poem like "Genesis" this process works because the poet's goal is not to examine his own self and past but to create an identity through the act of asserting artistic control over largely impersonal material. But in the early 1940s, in order to use memory effectively and develop an accurate sense of self, Roethke had to eliminate the formal techniques which led him to conventional stances.

Roethke's friend Robert Lowell encountered a similar problem with his own highly refined technique a decade later, eventually breaking away from form in *Life Studies*. Though the tradition of Allen Tate and the Fugitive poets with which Lowell struggled was different from the metaphysical tradition Roethke had embraced, Lowell's comments about the problem are illuminating:

> Poets of my generation and particularly younger ones have gotten terribly proficient at these forms. They write a very musical, difficult poem with tremendous skill, perhaps there's never been such skill. Yet the writing seems divorced from culture somehow. It's become too much something specialized that can't handle much experience. It's become a craft, purely a craft, and there must be some breakthrough back into life.[13]

Though Roethke was not much concerned about being "divorced from culture," he did feel that formal verse was incapable of handling the range of personal experience he wanted to examine. A reader today might see the change from formal to free verse as natural and relatively effortless, but Roethke's "breakthrough into life" was not as easy as we might think. Formal modes of writing were dominant in the 1940s, and Roethke had worked hard to become a skilled practitioner of the craft. Though Kenneth Burke and especially William Carlos Williams[14] praised and encouraged Roethke's move toward free verse, many of Roethke's early admirers had reservations. John Crowe Ransom found the greenhouse poems "not so much verse as very fine prose" (TR 148–10), and Yvor Winters said Roethke did not understand free verse (TR 14–24). Roethke certainly did not understand free verse in his first attempts at the new mode. "The Dug-Out" is an example:

> Steel
> Pressed against the hard brown earth
> Sharp edges and sharper points
> Hold back the winds
> Which whittle around the deep-dug furrow.
> Faces
> Rise from the hard brown earth,
> Hard white faces reaching out.
> But the dim eyes don't pierce
> The mist which now is covering everything.
> The sun
> Falling behind the far-off rocks
> Does not shine on the faces
> Which wait for the sign of a bird overhead
>
> (TR 19–18)

This rather oratorical prose, chopped into lines largely on the basis of syntax, does not succeed as free verse—or as any sort of poetic rendition of experience. Before he could move from the transitional work of a metrically loose, rhymed poem like "On the Road to Woodlawn" to the effective and accurate free verse of the greenhouse poems, Roethke had to make fundamental changes in the way he went about writing.

These changes in working methods began in the poet's notebooks. While Roethke's biographer Allan Seager exaggerates the differences between the notebooks of the '30s and those of the early '40s, his basic point, that the poet began to "loosen up" in the late '30s, is valid.[15] Even the earliest notebooks appear fragmentary and confusing, with drafts of different poems and parts of poems interspersed among teaching notes, addresses, fragments of letters, and other material. Like the later notebooks, they show evidence of Roethke's re-reading. But as the poet completes *Open House* and begins work on his second volume, the notebooks become even more confusing. For one thing, Roethke's work in them is much more extensive than earlier, involving not only a large increase in draft material for poems but many more prose fragments, questions, partial narratives, and other related material. The re-readings become more frequent, with corrections and additions of new work. In his new, more extensive use of the notebooks, Roethke spends a great deal of time describing aspects of the greenhouse, often without an idea of one particular poem in mind. One notebook from the early '40s contains several pages of such work, including details that find their way into "Root Cellar"— "All the breathing of growing"— "Weed Puller"— "Weeds beneath benches, / The drain-holes festooned with mossy roots dripping"— and "Transplanting"—"To be pinched and spun quick by the florists' green thumbs" (TR 36–87). The evocation of images from memory is more important than artifice here. I do not mean to imply that Roethke is unconcerned with the composition of specific poems at this point; we can see this passage eventually leading into work on "Forcing House." But the artifice here, the separation of greenhouse experience into distinct units that will become poems, arises gradually from the description instead of guiding and focussing the writing from the start. There is neither the rush to complete a formal unit, as in the early work, nor the clear sense of a particular subject, as in "On the Road to Woodlawn." "The poem invents the form; it insists on the form," Roethke writes in one notebook (TR 33–22). The poet's sense of artifice has become more organic; writing now involves discovery, not just conscious choice. There is still "form" here, Auden's "necessary order" latent in the experience, but Roethke has expanded his sense of what that form might be and is more willing to wait for it to reveal itself instead of rushing out to determine it at the start of the writing process. Roethke's belief in this period that "A poem becomes independent of you" (TR 33–22) shows a new attitude toward the self in writing, a movement away from will and stance toward a more subtle and fluid sense of himself and his material. The new type of preliminary work in the poet's notebooks reflects Roethke's growing awareness that it is vital to keep the gates of memory open, the self open to past experience.

Related to this new openness in the writing process is the value Roethke now places on what can perhaps best be defined as "looking." This concept first appears in the mid-'30s in a letter from Louise Bogan. Charging Roethke with a kind of fear of feeling in his early verse, she sent him a copy of Rilke's *Letters to a Young Poet* and advised, "... you will have to look at things until you don't know whether you are they or they are you" (TR 3–15, Bogan's emphasis). Roethke echoed this idea many years later in an interview for the film *In a Dark Time*, noting Rilke's careful observation of animals and referring to long, intense "looking" as "an extension of consciousness" (TR 140–1).[16] This "extension of consciousness," it is important to remember, arises not only from introspection, "looking" at the self, but also from close observation of entities outside the self. In the lengthy descriptive passages from the greenhouse notebooks we can see the poet "looking" as he writes. An example is Roethke's work on the memory of pulling weeds, which extends for more than a dozen pages (TR 35–68). The scene is examined again and again; details are repeated; and, though practically all of the images and phrases in "Weed Puller" appear in the passage, there is little attempt to order the material as it is being written. Roethke is not just gathering lines here as he might have done earlier—the work is too repetitious and extensive for that. Rather, he is intensely "looking" at a memory in an attempt to "extend his consciousness" to include elements of the greenhouse experience of his younger self, to go beyond simple description toward "seeing it imaginatively." What the poet eventually learns from this "looking" is revealed in the general comment about weed pulling he makes in a later notebook: "Ambivalent / Spirituality & sensuousness" (TR 35–65).

Though the greenhouse notebooks show that Roethke has moved away from conscious, limiting structures in his concepts of self and artifice, there is nonetheless a great deal of conscious work involved in the writing of the greenhouse poems. Roethke's comment on weed pulling is an example: After "looking" at the experience until his present sense of self begins to merge with aspects of the greenhouse and his past identity, the poet steps back from what he has written, examines it, and states what he has learned. The knowledge gained through this examination is then used in developing the artifice of the poem. This more conscious work comes after a given poem has begun to emerge from the mass of greenhouse notes; it signals a second stage in the compositional process. While it is necessary to discuss the preliminary greenhouse work with reference to several poems, as their origins are intermingled, the next stage in the writing process is best seen in the poet's work on a single poem. Here is the final text of "Cuttings" as it appeared in *The Lost Son and Other Poems:*

Cuttings

Sticks-in-a-drowse droop over sugary loam,
Their intricate stem-fur dries;
But still the delicate slips keep coaxing up water;
The small cells bulge;

One nub of growth
Nudges a sand-crumb loose,
Pokes through a musty sheath
Its pale tendrilous horn.

Like the second stage in the composition of an early poem, Roethke's work in completing a draft of "Cuttings" involves the development and selection of material to fit his idea of the artifice. In the early poems, of course, Roethke uses meter and rhyme as tools in the process, deleting material that does not fit the pattern and listing rhyme words as a kind of boundary within which new lines might be written. The absence of these tools in the composition of the greenhouse poems makes Roethke's task more difficult. The poet discusses this problem in "Some Remarks on Rhythm":

> We must realize, I think, that the writer in freer forms must have an even greater fidelity to his subject matter than the poet who has the support of form. He must keep his eye on the object, and his rhythm must move as a mind moves, must be imaginatively right, or he is lost. (SP 83)

As Jay Parini notes, Roethke is working with an essentially mimetic idea of free verse here, in which language is "exactly equivalent to reality."[17]

The difficulty of maintaining this equivalence is apparent in Roethke's notebook work on the greenhouse poems. Comparing the composition of "Genesis" with that of "Cuttings," we see in the later poem fewer lines completed and then revised for rhythmic regularity, more fragmentary beginnings which are not revised but just dropped. In one notebook passage, for example, there are more than twenty consecutive attempts at the third line of the poem (TR 36–74). It is clear from some of these fragments that Roethke knows the basic

movement he wants to develop at this transitional point in the poem—
the gradual transformation, within a continuous natural process, of
dormant stems into slips actively drawing up water—but he cannot
develop the details until he is satisfied with the beginning phrase of the
transition. Unlike Roethke's work on the individual stanzas of "Genesis," the completion of a part of "Cuttings" is bound up with the poet's
idea of the whole, his awareness that the clause beginning with "But"
is central to the poem's entire movement. Working toward a line that
is not formally metered but "imaginatively right," he repeats the opening "But" again and again, trying out different alternatives for the subject of the clause—"the sliced wedge of a stem," "the planted end,"
"the face"—in an attempt to start a train of thought and a corresponding rhythm which will carry him through this part of the poem.
Roethke's difficulty in getting past the beginning of the line at this
point reflects the fact that the process involved here is not a simple one
of summarizing or describing experience. It is an attempt, rather, to
re-create in the act of writing the movement of the poet's mind. In
"Genesis" and other early poems a tough personal stance arises
directly from Roethke's strict formal style and adamantine imagery,
but in the greenhouse poems this process is essentially reversed: The
imaginative attempt to relive the act of perception determines the lines
and phrases which make up the artifice; only when the poem's rhythms
"move as a mind moves," following the self in the process of perception and cognition, are they "imaginatively right."

The concrete details and perceptions we find in the finished poem
represent only a fraction of the total amount generated by Roethke's
intense observation of greenhouse experience. The final stage of composition, after the poet has completed a draft, involves careful selection of lines and images, along with revision and rearrangement of
material. The composition of "Cuttings" provides a clear example of
this kind of work, as the first draft of the poem is quite different from
the final text. Here is the draft, with its early title:

Propagation House

Slivers of stem, minutely furred,
Tucked into sand still marked with thumb-prints,
Cuttings of coleus, geranium, blood-red fuchsia
Stand stiff in their beds.

The topsoil crusts over like bakery sugar.

The delicate slips keep coaxing up water,
Bulging their flexible cells almost to bursting.
Even before fuzzy root-hairs reach for their gritty sustenance,
One pale horn of growth, a nubby root-cap,
Nudges a sand-crumb loose,
Humps like a sprout,
Then stretches out straight.

(TR 25–9)

"Propagation House" has the overall structure of "Cuttings," most of its details, and several of the specific images. But, compared to the final text, it is wordy and slow-moving. Such an overabundance of detail is a natural result of Roethke's reliance on memory and extensive "looking" in the early stages of composition. It is also related to the poet's shift from formal to free verse, as a letter from William Carlos Williams suggests:

> The thing sought is the essence and for this we need release in our technical and emotional resources, we need too security, confidence in the need to be saying (as poets!) what we are saying. But in releasing ourselves, in that feeling of confident release the difficulty is that we say too much, we say more than is distinctively ourselves, we slop over a little. (TR 14–23)

As Arnold Stein notes, the power of much of Roethke's poetry is based on "decisive acts of omission" which strengthen the remaining lines by replacing redundant material with "expressive" and "accurate" silences.[18] In paring down his draft to express no more than is "distinctively himself," Roethke uses what he has learned of himself and greenhouse experience in the earlier stages of writing to clarify and condense his material. In the case of "Weed Puller," for example, Roethke uses his discovery that the experience involved "Ambivalent/ Spirituality & sensuousness" (TR 35–65) to select the combination of sensuous images and spiritually oriented abstractions which will make up the finished poem.

Returning to "Cuttings," we find that the poet is most conscious of the artifice at this final stage of composition. Aesthetic concerns—

redundance, awkward rhythms, too many adjectives, irrelevant details—merge with Roethke's drive to present himself and his perceptions honestly and directly. Most of the first stanza, for example, is discarded because its specific flower names and references to transplanting detract from the focus of the poem and the experience. As we have seen from Roethke's early work on the transition in the third line of the published text, the gradual change from apparent lifelessness to the beginnings of growth is central to the poet's perception of the scene; the irrelevant material in the first stanza of "Propagation House" blurs this perception. Other details which distort the experience include the exaggeration of the phrase "almost to bursting" in line 7, the redundance of "flexible" in the same line and the appositive at the end of line 9, and the rather fussy effect produced by the accumulation of adjectives ending in "y" in lines 8 and 9. The rhythms of "Propagation House," with its abundance of unstressed syllables, lengthy lines, and feminine line endings, feel cluttered and overly elaborate. Roethke's goal in revising the draft is to pare the rhythms down, making them "natural," as he puts it (TR 16–15). In addition to removing these distorting, unnatural elements, Roethke tightens the structure of the poem to clarify the experience presented. The strong separation between the seemingly lifeless stems and the "slips coaxing up water" created by the stanza break in "Propagation House" is reduced in "Cuttings," in keeping with Roethke's sense of the change as part of a continuous natural process. In the final text the stanza break creates what Stein calls an "expressive" silence; it serves to emphasize the time between the drawing up of water and the first growth, reflecting the process more accurately. These revisions all show the "greater fidelity to his subject matter" Roethke develops in the third stage of composition.

The term "subject matter" should not be defined narrowly. In his letters to editors and friends in the mid-'40s, Roethke insisted that the greenhouse poems went "beyond mere description" (TR 148–9) of natural phenomena and suggested "at least two levels of experience" (TR 16–14). The level beneath that of greenhouse description includes Roethke's presentation of self in the sequence. "Cuttings," the shortest and least anthropomorphic of the greenhouse poems, presents something of a special case here: The second level is not brought out in the poem itself but rather through the interaction between "Cuttings" and the poem which follows it in the sequence and shares its title,

"Cuttings (*later*)." While "Cuttings" has its origins in the poet's observation of a natural process, "Cuttings (*later*)"— even in its early
stages—involves the relation between nature and the self. Here is the
text as it appeared in *The Lost Son and Other Poems:*

> *Cuttings*
> (later)
>
> This urge, wrestle, resurrection of dry sticks,
> Cut stems struggling to put down feet,
> What saint strained so much,
> Rose on such lopped limbs to a new life?
>
> I can hear, underground, that sucking and sobbing,
> In my veins, in my bones I feel it,—
> The small waters seeping upward,
> The tight grains parting at last.
> When sprouts break out,
> Slippery as fish,
> I quail, lean to beginnings, sheath-wet.

As we might expect from the subject and images—"sticks," water,
and "sheath"— common to both poems, Roethke worked on "Cuttings" and "Cuttings (*later*)" simultaneously. Both poems were
largely composed in 1944, although, like most of the greenhouse
poems, they include details which appeared earlier in the undifferentiated greenhouse material of the notebooks. As I mentioned, the connection between nature and the self is at the core of "Cuttings (*later*)"
from the beginning, but in bringing the piece to its final state Roethke
makes the poem more specifically personal, moving from this rather
rhetorical version of the concluding stanza—

> Who could shun this hump and scratch,
> The close sweat of growth,
> Not quail to the same itch,
> Not stir, lean to beginnings, sheath-wet?
>
> (TR 18–60)—

to a stanza which anchors the link with nature firmly in the experience of "I," the poet himself, and expresses it not as a question but as an affirmative statement. While the connection between self and nature is clarified in the revisions of "Cuttings (*later*)," it is deliberately excluded from "Cuttings." In one instance, Roethke uses details from the draft material of "Cuttings (*later*)" to revise the other poem from its "Propagation House" stage. The opening line of "Cuttings" appears among this draft material as "The best of me droops, in a drowse" (TR 35–67). In reworking this line, Roethke removes the personal pronoun from the material, keeping "Cuttings" focussed on nature, not the self. The fact that "Cuttings" concentrates on description without a perceiving "I" is no accident. As Jarold Ramsey notes, Roethke "suppresses all possible human implications" in "Cuttings" in order to establish an objective perspective.[19] In doing this, the poet asserts that the connection between self and nature comes from close observation of greenhouse life and is not applied to the material from the beginning in a kind of arbitrary analogy . The "two levels" Roethke develops in the greenhouse poems are connected organically, as "looking"—even if not specifically directed toward the self—is intrinsically linked to an "extension of consciousness." In their position as the opening poems of the greenhouse sequence, "Cuttings" and "Cuttings (*later*)" clearly announce the relation between natural processes and the development of identity which is at the heart of the sequence and the volume as a whole.

In a statement made at Northwestern University in 1963 Roethke characterized the title poem of *Open House* as "a clumsy, innocent, desperate asseveration" and contrasted it to his subsequent work:

> The spirit or soul—should we say the self, once perceived, *becomes* the soul?—this I was keeping "spare" in my desire for the essential. But the spirit need not be spare: it can grow gracefully and beautifully like a tendril, like a flower. (SP 21, Roethke's emphasis)

In working toward this organic sense of self, Roethke went through basic changes in the way he wrote. In the late '30s and early '40s he began to rely more on memory and extensive "looking" at objects and experiences as a way of generating poetic material. Rhyme, meter, and even the awareness of artifice itself were downplayed as Roethke examined his past, attempting to re-create the process of perception in the act of writing. Dropping the support of formal verse, he worked toward rhythms which would "move as a mind moves" and a corresponding new sense of self: The artificial stance assumed in the early poems is replaced by a consciousness, open to experience, which grows in the process of writing and leads to an accurate expression of personal identity in the finished text. In a notebook kept as he was completing the greenhouse poems, Roethke wrote, "You must learn to walk before you can dance; you can't be a master of suggestion unless you are a master of description" (TR 34–45). The greenhouse poems are descriptive in the richest sense of the term. "Learning to walk" in these poems was, for Roethke, an essential prelude to the "dance" of more complex self-discovery in the "Lost Son" sequence.

CHAPTER FOUR

"The Method Is Cyclic":
The "Lost Son" Sequence and
Praise to the End!

If Roethke became a "master of description" in his composition of the greenhouse poems of the early '40s, his work during the rest of the decade was focussed on developing powers of "suggestion." The four-poem "Lost Son" sequence which concludes Roethke's second book is the first manifestation of this new development. While the greenhouse poems lead to self-discovery through the examination of specific memories, the later work is concerned with underlying patterns behind the memories; in it Roethke begins to delve directly into the unconscious, without the mediation of greenhouse description. The result is complex, highly experimental work unlike anything Roethke had done before. In Chapter 5 we will take a close look at the new ways of writing behind an example of this work, but first it is necessary to consider the material as a whole. The four-poem "Lost Son" group is the first of the sequences of longer poems which become increasingly important in Roethke's career, including *Praise to the End!, Meditations of an Old Woman,* and *North American Sequence.* It is also the only group of poems to be incorporated in two separate volumes: as the conclusion of *The Lost Son and Other Poems* in 1948 and as the opening of Part II of *Praise to the End!* in 1951. In Roethke's development of the "Lost Son" poems and *Praise to the End!* as sequences we can see the overall process of self-discovery he underwent from the mid-'40s to the early '50s.

Writing about "The Lost Son" in his essay "Open Letter," Roethke summarizes the general movement of the poem and the sequences in which it is included:

> This crude account tells very little about what actually happens
> in the poem; but at least you can see that the method is cyclic. I
> believe that to go forward as a spiritual man it is necessary first to go
> back. Any history of the psyche (or allegorical journey) is bound to
> be a succession of experiences, similar yet dissimilar. There is a
> perpetual slipping-back, then a going-forward; but there is *some*
> "progress." Are not some experiences so powerful and so profound
> (I am not speaking of the merely compulsive) that they repeat them-
> selves, thrust themselves upon us, again and again, with variation
> and change, each time bringing us closer to our own most particular
> (and thus most universal) reality? We go, as Yeats said, from
> exhaustion to exhaustion. To begin from the depths and come out—
> that is difficult; for few know where the depths are or can recognize
> them; or, if they do, are afraid. (SP 39–40, Roethke's emphasis)

The two-level description of the greenhouse poems points to the
"depths" Roethke mentions here in its connections between the self
and the primal world of natural processes. The drive toward "beginnings" Roethke announces in "Cuttings (*later*)" leads the poet back to
the "slippery grave" ("Weed Puller") where life starts and ends, and
Roethke's original title for the greenhouse poems, "News of the Root"
(SL 113), suggests a thorough examination of these depths. But in
1945 Roethke complained that the greenhouse poems were "not suf-
ficiently related" (SL 113). The greenhouse experience is obviously
one of the "powerful" ones Roethke mentions in "Open Letter," and
we see its repetition "with variation and change" in each poem. But the
greenhouse poems do not, in the end, develop a "*succession* of experiences" that would reveal a "history of the psyche." Though some critics have since found broad patterns in the greenhouse poems— a
progression from physical description to meditation, "a general sense
of growth," a movement toward transcendence of the past[1]—
Roethke's own dissatisfaction with the relations among the greenhouse poems led him toward a much more deliberate concept of progression in the "Lost Son" sequence. If the greenhouse poems are like
separate photographs of memories carefully arranged in an album, the
"Lost Son" sequence is like a movie.[2] The sequence of longer, multi-
sectioned poems allows the poet to undertake a kind of "journey" in

the process of writing, to extend his self-discovery beyond the bounds of specific scenes and memories.

This extended self-discovery involved changes not only in the idea of progression among poems but also in style. While the two-level nature of the greenhouse poems anchors the poet's discoveries about himself in images from the natural world, the sequences of Roethke's middle period are considerably more dense symbolically, with more complex relations between the physical and psychological dimensions. As Roethke moved from "description" to "suggestion," he began to work more "intuitively," as he put it (SL 142); and the result is poems which develop a whole range of suggestions in different images. A worm, for example, functions simultaneously as a literal creature used for fish bait, an archetype of mortality, a phallic symbol, and an image of regression and lowliness. This associative richness, with its abundance of psychosexual connotations, reflects Roethke's extensive forays into "the depths" of the unconscious, which we will see in more detail in Chapter 5. In the completed texts, the wealth of suggestions is augmented by the poet's predominant interest in what he called "dramatic" expression in this period. In the greenhouse poems Roethke wanted to "be true to the actual" (SL 119), but his development of the poems in the sequences as dramatic pieces changed the context of images considerably:

> All these states of mind were to be rendered dramatically, without comment, without allusion, the action often implied or indicated in the interior monologue or dialogue between the self and its mentor, or conscience, or, sometimes, another person. (SP 10)

By removing comments, allusions, and direct action in the physical world in his drive for the dramatic, the poet creates difficult, often disjointed work in which images are liberated from their standard contexts. Meaning is expressed in a fundamentally new way, as Roethke notes in "Open Letter":

> If intensity has compressed the language so it seems, on early reading, obscure, this obscurity should break open suddenly for the serious reader who can hear the language: the "meaning" itself should come as a dramatic revelation, an excitement. The clues will be scattered richly—as life scatters them; the symbols will mean what

they usually mean—and sometimes something more. (SP 42)

This new, more suggestive approach is vital to the poet's more complex self-discovery in the sequences. With it, Roethke is able to develop, as he put it, "a genuine imaginative order out of what comes from the unconscious" (SL 129).

As Roethke noted in the seminar on identity, "The human problem is to find out what one really *is:* whether one exists, whether existence is possible. But how?" (SP 20, Roethke's emphasis). The greenhouse memories respond to the first part of this comment, showing the poet "what he *is*"; in the sequences that follow these poems, Roethke goes on to consider the broader question of "whether existence is possible" for him. The sequences trace what Roethke called the "mental and spiritual crisis" (SL 114) of confronting his own experience, of integrating the world of the greenhouse— including his father's death and his own maturation— into a clear sense of his identity in the present. The process of engaging the past and incorporating discoveries from it in a deeper sense of self is at the heart of Roethke's work on the "Lost Son" sequence and *Praise to the End!* "To begin from the depths and come out" was his overall goal. As the sequences take shape we can see the poet gradually moving toward a resolution of his confrontation with the past.

Roethke's work of the mid to late '40s divides roughly into two periods: from 1945 to the fall of 1947, during which he composed the four-poem sequence included in *The Lost Son* while teaching at Bennington and Pennsylvania State; and from fall of '47, when Roethke moved to the University of Washington, to the completion of *Praise to the End!* in 1950. Within these two periods the poet developed the sequences in several stages. First came a three-poem version of the "Lost Son" sequence, without "A Field of Light." This was followed by the four-poem version published in *The Lost Son*. In late 1947 Roethke completed the title poem of *Praise to the End!* He then went on to the eight other new poems in this book, conceiving them as a single sequence in the following order: "Where Knock Is Open Wide"; "I Need, I Need"; "Bring the Day!"; "Give Way, Ye Gates"; "Sensibility! O La!"; "O Lull Me, Lull Me"; "Unfold! Unfold!" and "I Cry, Love! Love!" The last stage of Roethke's work involved dividing this group into Parts I and II of the finished text and integrating the original "Lost Son" sequence in the new volume. Looking at these stages in order, we can see how Roethke's understanding of himself and his past evolved in the process of writing.

As "Open Letter" explains, Roethke's progress on this journey of self-discovery is "cyclic." This cyclic quality is reflected in the repeating five-part structure Roethke uses for three of the four poems in the "Lost Son" sequence. The pattern of self-exploration in "The Lost Son," described in detail in "Open Letter," involves an initial sense of stagnation, flight from it, regression to an irrational level, then re-creation of a childhood greenhouse experience, leading to a more satisfying vision of self and world. This pattern is followed, with some variation, in the two poems written immediately after "The Lost Son": "The Long Alley" and "The Shape of the Fire." "The Lost Son," "The Long Alley," and "The Shape of the Fire" were all completed by February, 1947 and represent Roethke's first sense of the sequence; in a letter at this time he wrote that the finished manuscript of his new book contained only "three long poems."[3] This first group of three poems is a highly coherent unit which exemplifies the kind of cyclic progress Roethke describes in his essay. Though the process of self-discovery is repeated in each poem, the poet's self-understanding increases as the sequence progresses; he gradually becomes more aware of how the process works, more confident of its final outcome. From a state of calm expectation— "Wait"— at the end of "The Lost Son" (5. 25), Roethke moves toward self-acceptance and a desire for active confrontation with reality—"I'll take the fire"—in "The Long Alley" (5. 10), and then on to what Louis Martz calls "full maturity and conscious power"[4] in "The Shape of the Fire." The titles of the three poems, all from the world of the greenhouse, reflect this movement: The poet starts out as a "Lost Son," then perceives "The Long Alley" ahead of him, and finally comes to know "The Shape of the Fire" at the heart of the greenhouse and his past.

Added to the "Lost Son" sequence in the fall of 1947, "A Field of Light" involves the same general movement from a sense of personal stagnation to a new vision of self, but there are several important differences between this poem and the three composed before it. Unlike the other "Lost Son" poems, "A Field of Light" is written entirely in the past tense; it thus seems less dramatic and chaotic than the other works. The title of the poem does not suggest the intensity of the enclosed greenhouse, as do the others, but rather a sense of freedom and spiritual illumination in the open field. In fact, the specific greenhouse experiences which surface in the fourth sections of the other poems are completely absent from "A Field of Light." The five-part structure is replaced by a more compact three-part organization which leaves no room for a long, irrational "Gibber" ("The Lost Son," Part 3) or a "Return" ("The Lost Son," Part 4) to the greenhouse. The stress in the later poem is not so much on the process of self-discovery as on the vision of self attained after the process is completed. In contrast to the other poems, "A Field of Light" has its longest, most developed section at the end, in which we see a man at peace with himself and nature:

> I could watch! I could watch!
> I saw the separateness of all things!
> My heart lifted up with the great grasses;
> The weeds believed me, and the nesting birds.
> There were clouds making a rout of shapes crossing a
>   windbreak of cedars,
> And a bee shaking drops from a rain-soaked honeysuckle.
> The worms were delighted as wrens.
> And I walked, I walked through the light air;
> I moved with the morning.
>
> (3. 14–22)

All of these differences suggest an increased distance on Roethke's part from his past and a slight movement away from the regressive and irrational aspects of his personality. These changes may reflect the temporary therapeutic effect of completing the original three-poem sequence. Roethke was certainly aware of the potential for psychic progress through writing. Commenting on his work in 1955, he described his poems as an attempt to "transmute and purify my 'life,' the sense of being defiled by it" (SP 15). "A Field of Light" seems a more "purified" poem than the ones written before it. The differences between "A Field of Light" and the other three poems may also reflect changes in Roethke's life. During the two-year period in which the first three poems were written, Roethke spent a great deal of time in his hometown. He worked there on the original "Lost Son" sequence in the summer of 1945 and from January, 1946 until the completion of the three-poem series in February of the following year. A few entries from the poet's notebooks of this period suggest the kind of immersion in his past Roethke was undergoing during the months in Saginaw:

> Long, fruitless introspection, characteristic of the German, relieved
> by occasional dim flickers of insight. Like a half-blind animal that at
> best can see no colors but gray, he broods and broods.
>
> My memory, my prison.
>
> I am nothing but what I remember.
>
> What was the greenhouse? It was a jungle, and it was paradise; it
> was order and disorder: Was it an escape? No, for it was a reality
> harsher than reality.
>
> The long mind roves back.
> I wear between my eyes the image of death.
> I carry death in my mouth.
>
> Blundering man, gentle with birds,
> Whom the caterpillar caressed,
> Whom the snake kissed.
>
> I was never his son, not I.[5]

In his notebooks the poet constantly examines his memories, trying to
determine his true relation to the greenhouse, to his father, to aspects
of himself. Even the process of memory itself is called into question.
This is a considerably more intense process than the "looking" at the
past Roethke had done in the greenhouse notebooks; it involves not
only gathering material from the past but critically judging it and trying to determine its meaning. Memories are developed not so much as
narratives important in their own right but as tools for self-scrutiny. As
we will see in the next chapter, Roethke works continuously at liberating unconscious material in these notebooks, not just remembering
events but actually creating whole worlds of psychic imagery from his
plunges into "the depths." This kind of intense introspection was often
painful for Roethke, as the reference to "my memory, my prison" and
the description of himself as a "half-blind animal" suggest.

In addition to this immersion in the past, Roethke suffered his second mental breakdown during this period—after Christmas, 1945—

which may be reflected in some of the more irrational parts of the sequence. However, it is important not to exaggerate the role of Roethke's breakdowns in his poetic work. To compare Roethke with Sylvia Plath and Rimbaud, as one critic does,[6] is to romanticize mental derangement and reduce these poets' vastly different work to a form of inspired—or induced—madness. To suggest that writing about himself was psychologically "dangerous" for Roethke, as another critic does,[7] is romanticization of a different sort which conjures up a distorted image of the poet as martyr to his own sensitivities. Roethke's biographer Allan Seager gives a plausible interpretation when he suggests that the five-part structure developed in "The Lost Son" reflects the pattern of the poet's breakdown, with the second and third sections expressing "the terror, the physical and psychic exhaustion of his stay in the hospital." But Seager goes too far in implying that Roethke's mental illness provided the "substructure" for the entire poem.[8] Neither "The Lost Son" nor the other two poems in the group I have been discussing describe or arise directly from Roethke's breakdown. Rather, they are based primarily on an intense imaginative reliving of the past, as Roethke's comments in notebooks and the essay "Open Letter" make clear.

"A Field of Light" was written during a much calmer period in the poet's life, the summer of 1947, a month of which Roethke spent at the Yaddo Writer's Conference in rural New York. Roethke's physical distance from Saginaw and his past, the relaxed atmosphere of Yaddo, and the friendship and support of other writers, notably Robert Lowell, are reflected in the brighter, more peaceful tone of the poem Roethke eventually came to see as an "interlude" in the "Lost Son" sequence (SL 142). Roethke's decision to insert this "interlude" in a group of poems he had originally considered complete is a choice which suggests an increased sense of control over the personal material from which the poems are derived. With "A Field of Light" added, the sequence no longer reflects its own chronological development in Roethke's life; a re-ordering of personal experience is involved. This re-ordering implies an ability to see how the sequence presents the self and a desire to arrange that presentation in a certain way.

Though the last of the four "Lost Son" poems to be written, "A Field of Light," is more self-accepting than the others, Roethke is not satisfied with the kind of "progress" involved here. If he were, he would have kept the poems in their order of composition, concluding the series with the least "troubled" of the four. Roethke's final arrangement of the sequence links the later vision of self in "A Field of Light" back to the poems which gave rise to it and changes it from an endpoint to an interlude in a cycle. Kenneth Burke summarizes the value of this kind of cycle-making in "The Vegetal Radicalism of Theodore Roethke":

> The dangers inherent in the regressive imagery seem to have received an impetus from without, that drove the poet still more forcefully in the same direction, dipping him in the river who loved water. His own lore thus threatened to turn against him. The enduring of such discomforts is a "birth" in the sense that, if the poet survives the ordeal, he is essentially stronger, and has to this extent *forged himself* an identity. [Burke's emphasis][9]

What new sense of identity has Roethke developed by inserting "A Field of Light" in the "Lost Son" sequence? The self we see in the completed sequence seems less troubled, less obsessed with specific childhood experiences than it does in the original three-poem series. The intensity built up in the first version of the sequence through repeated patterns in structure, style and subject matter is now interrupted by a poem that offers what Louis Martz calls "a retrospective view of the development of the entire sequence."[10] "A Field of Light" shows the enlightenment and ease toward which the sequence as a whole has been headed.

Inserted in the middle of the group, this "retrospective view" adds a suggestion that the poet will eventually be able to put the intense experiences of the earlier poems into perspective. At a future time he will presumably see these psychic processes in the relatively calm way he looks at them in "A Field of Light," and in retrospect the most vivid aspects will not be the "dark" ones—the terror, the irrationality, the regression to childhood—but the "light" at the end of the experience. The position of "A Field of Light" between the second and third poems of the original sequence also modifies the structure of the group, setting up a new balance between two poems focussing on "darkness"— "The Lost Son" and "The Long Alley"—and two poems focussing on "light"—"A Field of Light" and "The Shape of the Fire." Though this re-ordering of the poems does not eliminate the "darker" passages in the concluding work, the inclusion of a new poem in the sequence "brightens" the group as a whole. Stressing in "A Field of Light" that the final illumination, not flight or regression, is the most lasting part of the process of self-discovery, Roethke makes the affirmative vision at the end of the four-poem sequence all the more powerful.

The addition of "A Field of Light" to the middle of the "Lost Son" sequence is the first major step in Roethke's cyclic progress. The self-discovery involved here comes not from new understanding of a specific memory, as it had in the greenhouse poems, or from progressive repetition of a pattern of psychic development, as it had in the first three "Lost Son" poems, but from complex interactions among the different sides of the poet's experience seen in the works. "A Field of Light" comments on the other poems in the sequence from the distance of its retrospective vision; but this vision, set in the middle of the group, is then modified by its new role as an "interlude" rather than a summary. Cycle-making of this sort demands constant re-evaluation of poems and the experiences they describe. This includes returns to the "depths" even after they seem to have been left behind, in the "perpetual slipping-back" that is part of the cyclic process. Burke's "birth" metaphor is appropriate for this intense, laborious process. In a reading of the four-poem "Lost Son" sequence, Roethke mentioned that the last poem of the group, "The Shape of the Fire," was originally an attempt to conclude the exhausting process of self-exploration he had been undergoing as he was writing these works.[11]

This attempt was not successful. By the fall of 1947 Roethke had completed the four-poem "Lost Son" sequence and had begun teaching at the University of Washington. *The Lost Son and Other Poems* was due to be published the following year, but the poet was still immersed in the cyclic process of self-discovery he had begun two years earlier. Its first manifestation after the move to Washington was the poem "Praise to the End!" Commenting on this piece in a letter to Kenneth Burke, Roethke stresses its close thematic relation to the "Lost Son" sequence:

> I've just finished a long (97 lines) poem, the last probably from the dark world. The tone of some of the passages is somewhat the same; but what is said (dramatically) is different. The thing is much "clearer," I think, than the other: can really be worked at as equations: There's a more complicated "ecstasy" passage, which resolves into death–wish. (SL 147)

Though "Praise to the End!" in its final version has four sections, an explanatory outline Roethke provided for it suggests the five-part structure of the three original "Lost Son" poems:

1) Act
2) Reaction to act (quiet, sense of impotence)
3) Song: reasons for act
      reaction again
4) Two flashbacks related to act, then the present again
5) Sublimation (The fact that there are few human symbols here isn't accidental.)[12]

The middle sections here seem particularly close to the earlier five-part model, including the sense of exhaustion in the second section, the irrational song of the third part, and the regressive flashbacks in the fourth part. From these similarities it might seem that "Praise to the End!" represents a return to the obsessions of the first three "Lost Son" poems, and that Roethke, in effect, learned nothing from his composition and arrangement of the four-poem sequence. However, the differences between "Praise to the End!" and the "Lost Son" sequence indicate some important developments in the poet's understanding.

Though Burke's "Vegetal Radicalism" essay provides an excellent analysis of the *Lost Son* volume, his assertion that "Praise to the End!" and other poems written directly after *The Lost Son* "repeat the regressive imagery without the abysmal anguish"[13] undervalues the persistent element of despair in some of these works. The cause for this despair can be seen in the "equation" Roethke felt summarized "Praise to the End!": "onanism equals death" (SP 40). Unlike the "Lost Son" poems, "Praise to the End!" begins not with general stagnation but with a specific masturbatory "act." The poet's reactions to this act—despair, flight into irrationality, regression—are reminiscent of the "Lost Son" sequence, but the final ecstasy is now seen as a "death-wish." The return to the past in Part 3, instead of refreshing the poet and leading him to a revitalized sense of self, now involves him with "graves" (3. 25), "ghosts" (3. 28), "owls" (3. 21), and dreams of being "all bones" (3. 13) as the father's death looms imminently over adolescent experience. In "Praise to the End!" the past is not a greenhouse but a grave.

The despair underlying "Praise to the End!" also colors the father's presence in the poem. The role of the dead father as a judgmental figure—"Father Fear," as Roethke calls him—had been hinted at in the "Gibber" section of "The Lost Son" (3. 16–17). In "Praise to the End!" this aspect becomes dominant, as the poet begs mercy for his autoerotic transgression: "Father, forgive my hands" (1. 12). But the father also has a benign side: his role as a loving guide who can help the son in his progress toward maturity. This ambivalent vision of the father is at the heart of the two sequences. While the judging father arises from the son's masturbatory guilt and is bound up with a death-wish, the loving father represents the hope of successful progress toward resolution of the problems of identity and sexuality. When the judging father appears, the poet is mired in his own failures, the bleak world of onanism and death. The loving father, in contrast, is a model who can lead the poet from masturbation toward genuine love, from fear and guilt toward a renewed sense of self. In the "Lost Son" sequence as a whole the potentially destructive aspect of the father is gradually overshadowed by his nurturing abilities, and he becomes a "lively understandable spirit" ("The Lost Son," 5. 21) who can guide the poet to a kind of maturity. But in "Praise to the End!" these positive qualities are gone; the poet must beg forgiveness of a "Father of tensions" (1. 4), a "ghost" (1. 11) whose condemning presence leads him eventually toward death.

The change in the role of the father from the "Lost Son" sequence to "Praise to the End!" reveals some basic limitations in the final resolution of the four-poem sequence. The incompleteness of the vision of self attained in the "Lost Son" group is dramatized by the contrast between the last four lines of the sequence—

To know that light falls and fills, often without our knowing,
As an opaque vase fills to the brim from a quick pouring,
Fills and trembles at the edge yet does not flow over,
Still holding and feeding the stem of the contained flower.
("The Shape of the Fire," 5. 15–18)—

and these lines from the beginning of "Praise to the End!":

The rings have gone from the pond.
The river's alone with its water.

All risings
Fall.

(I. 13–16)

In the first passage the stress is on containment, security, constant nurturing; the long lines with their smooth, regular rhythms and the half-
rhymes at the ends of the lines augment this emphasis. The lines from
"Praise to the End!" illustrate a situation in which this security breaks
down; the enclosing "rings" of the calm "pond" are gone, and the
"river" takes over, breaking the smooth order of the verse form as it
pushes toward a "Fall." The "river" here is clearly sexual and points
to a problem which is not adequately resolved in the "Lost Son"
sequence.

Though "The Lost Son" and other poems in the sequence hint at
sexual activities in references to "serpents" ("The Long Alley," I. I),
"eels," "mouths of jugs" ("The Lost Son," I. 55, 3. 22), and other
suggestive images, sexuality generally remains on the level of infantile fantasy in these poems. Though masturbation is mentioned, the
conflict between easy autoerotic gratification and the desire for sex
with another person does not predominate; and the fact that the poet is
by himself in the ecstatic scene at the end of the sequence seems to
have no negative connotations. However, when more adult sexual
needs are considered in "Praise to the End!" the absence of another
person in the concluding vision of self is connected with onanism and
death. Roethke mentions this in his letter to Kenneth Burke:

> I've been astonished to find that in the last 24 lines of affirmation
> there is not one reference to anything human except the line:
>
> "I've crawled from the mire, alert as a saint or a dog."
>
> And a saint is hardly human. All the other images are fish, birds,
> animals, etc…Onan's folly. (SL 147, Roethke's ellipsis)

In another letter he refers to the union with nature at the end of the
poem—a union which is similar in tone and imagery to that at the end
of "A Field of Light" or "The Shape of the Fire"—as "Ecstasy-death
wish, etc. (Sublimation carried to its ultimate end)" (SL 152). The
ecstatic vision of harmony becomes, like masturbation, a flight from

confronting real sexual needs and a disobedience of the father. While the nurturing father in the "Lost Son" sequence leads the poet toward personal security and self-acceptance, the judging father in "Praise to the End!" shows what Roethke has *not* achieved: intimate relations outside the self. The poet's first response to this new challenge is flight and a longing for death.

Though "Praise to the End!" depicts a failure to attain a level of social and sexual maturity, the conclusion of this work is not completely hopeless. In "Open Letter" Roethke says the following about the end of the poem:

> Is the protagonist "happy" in his death-wish? Is he a mindless euphoric jigger who goes blithering into oblivion? No. In terms of the whole sequence, he survives: this is a dead-end explored. His self-consciousness, his very will to live saves him from the *annihilation* of the ecstasy. (SP 40–41, Roethke's emphasis)

"Self-consciousness" and a "will to live" are qualities the poet has gained by the end of the "Lost Son" sequence. Though the self-acceptance achieved here gives the poet the confidence to "explore" masturbation and its consequences, Roethke eventually comes to consider the attempt to deal with sexual needs exclusively through the self-oriented vision of the "Lost Son" sequence a "dead-end." The cyclic process of self-discovery involves continual re-thinking of previous conclusions in this way. As Roethke noted in "Open Letter," each poem is "complete in itself; yet each in a sense is a stage" (SP 37). As former endpoints become stages in a cycle, the poet's awareness of self grows. "Transcend that vision. What is first or early is easy to believe. But... it may enchain you" [Roethke's ellipsis], the poet wrote in a notebook during this period.[14] "Praise to the End!" points out a kind of enchainment in self, in which the sexual excitement of the "duke of eels" (1. 8) is always followed by a sense of despair, impotence and death, a feeling of being "asleep in a bower of dead skin" (2. 31), and "All risings / Fall" (1. 15–16). Later poems will attempt to transcend this lonely pattern of arousal and sorrow. This transcendence, however, does not involve discarding the earlier sense of self but rather including it in a newer, broader vision.

Written after "Praise to the End!" in 1949–1950, the remaining eight poems in Roethke's third book were conceived originally as a sequence tracing the poet's growth from early childhood to maturity.[15] A letter indicates that the six-poem sequence making up Part I of the published text at first also included "Unfold! Unfold!" and "I Cry, Love! Love!" (SL 155). Later these two poems were removed from the sequence and placed at the end of Part II. In February, 1949 Roethke sent a draft of the first poem of the group, "Where Knock Is Open Wide," to Kenneth Burke, outlining his initial plans for the eight-poem sequence in a letter:

> This piece is conceived as the first of a sequence of dramatic pieces beginning with a small child and working up. A kind of tensed-up *Prelude,* maybe: no comment; everything in the mind of the kid. (SL 148)

The title "Praise to the End!" is from *The Prelude* and suggests an interesting link between the new sequence and the poem Roethke wrote just before it.[16] Here are the lines from which this title is taken:

> How strange that all
> The terrors, pains, and early miseries,
> Regrets, vexations, lassitudes interfused
> Within my mind, should e'er have borne a part,
> And that a needful part, in making up
> The calm existence that is mine when I
> Am worthy of myself! Praise to the end!
> Thanks to the means which Nature deigned to employ;
> Whether her fearless visitings, or those
> That came with soft alarm, like hurtless light
> Opening the peaceful clouds; or she may use
> Severer interventions, ministry
> More palpable, as best might suit her aim.
> (Book I, 344–356, 1850 edition)[17]

Referring to the title in another letter, Roethke tells Burke that "Ambiguities, ironical and otherwise, are intended" (SL 151). Wordsworth's confident, assertive lines stand in clear contrast to a poem in which "Praise to the end!" becomes a death-wish.

Though Wordsworth's position is treated ironically in Roethke's poem, the lines from *The Prelude* also suggest a goal for Roethke:

self-acceptance and harmony with nature. The first attainment of this goal at the end of the "Lost Son" sequence was shattered by the emergence of powerful sexual needs in "Praise to the End!" In the "tensed-up *Prelude*" which follows it, the poet attempts to trace his own sexual development as he dramatically reconstructs "The terrors, pains, and early miseries" of childhood and adolescence. The cyclic development of the sequence takes another turn here. In a misjudgment typical of his work on sequences, Roethke had believed "Praise to the End!" to be the last poem "from the dark world" (SL 147). But the new issues this poem raised sent him back again for new answers. This return to the past is an extended and more self-critical version of the returns in the "Lost Son" poems; it puts the past we have seen in the earlier sequence under a microscope by separating it into different periods and focussing more directly on the sexual issues raised by "Praise to the End!" The fact that the new sequence is made up entirely of dramatic monologues gives Roethke's encounter with the past an added intensity. He is not only returning to childhood as he had earlier but actually reliving it, speaking with the child's voice as he seeks to express everything "in the mind of the kid." This more intense and detailed treatment of past experience represents for Roethke another step in the cyclic progress toward "The calm existence that is mine when I / Am worthy of myself!"

The eight-poem "tensed-up *Prelude*" breaks naturally into four units. Roethke published the second, third and fourth poems of the series under the single title "Give Way, Ye Gates" in 1950. At the conclusion of this group he added the following note:

> I wish to have these three poems considered as an entity, the group making one poem from childhood into a violent adolescence: a caterwauling.[18]

If this three-poem group is taken as the core of the sequence, the opening poem of the volume, "Where Knock Is Open Wide," takes the sequence back from "childhood" toward infancy, while "Sensibility! O La!" and "O Lull Me, Lull Me" move forward from "violent adolescence" toward young adulthood. The last two poems of the sequence, "Unfold! Unfold!" and "I Cry, Love! Love!," represent an adult perspective, which helps explain why Roethke eventually separated them from the rest of the series. Briefly, the first four poems of the sequence trace the child's development from infantile confusion and fear of his parents' power—

> A kitten can
> Bite with his feet;
> Papa and Mamma
> Have more teeth.
>
> ("Where Knock Is Open Wide," 1. 1–4)—

through the first awareness of his own independent sexuality— "I know another fire. / Has roots." ("I Need, I Need," 4. 15–16)—with its attendant anxieties; to a sense of sexual readiness— "It's time to begin!" ("Bring the Day!," 3. 7)—based on a faith that "What slides away"—parental nurturing, a childhood sense of security—will, in the end, "provide" ("Give Way, Ye Gates," 4. 16–17). The next two poems examine the autoerotic stage of "John-of-the-thumb" ("Sensibility! O La!," 2. 4) as the young man develops a clearer sense of self and other through sexual fantasies. The last two poems depict conflicts in the adult between a genuine desire to love and the death-wish derived from guilt Roethke noted earlier in "Praise to the End!"

The arrangement of the poems for the completed volume is the last stage in Roethke's cyclic progress. When it was published in 1951, *Praise to the End!* was divided into two sections: Part I contained the first six poems in the "tensed-up *Prelude*" while Part II included the "Lost Son" sequence, followed by "Praise to the End!," "Unfold! Unfold!," and "I Cry, Love! Love!" As I mentioned, Roethke originally wrote "Unfold! Unfold!" and "I Cry, Love! Love!" as the concluding part of the eight-poem "tensed-up *Prelude*," but these poems have enough similarities to the "Lost Son" series and "Praise to the End!" that they do not stand out awkwardly in Part II of the finished volume. Both poems are written from an adult perspective, and we see in both the old progression from stagnation, through regression, to a new vision of self. Stylistically these two poems are indistinguishable from the others in Part II; the short lines and singsong rhythms that mark the early poems in the sequence gradually disappear as the series progresses. Richard Blessing points to these stylistic and thematic similarities among the poems of Part II:

Poem after poem begins with the thought of death and with the language of death.... The voice is anxious, the sentences terse and frequently truncated, without subjects. The imagery is oppressive, establishing a kind of wasteland as spiritual landscape. But out of such beginnings the poet sets about making a verbal gesture of cherishing, a gesture celebrating life and its motion.[19]

In their position at the end of Part II in the finished volume, "Unfold! Unfold!" and "I Cry, Love! Love!" complete this "gesture," capping the volume and linking both sections. They respond to the insufficiencies "Praise to the End!" revealed in the "Lost Son" sequence by going beyond the vision of self-acceptance at the conclusion of "The Shape of the Fire" to include a new understanding of sex and death.

We can see this new attitude in the secure, assertive tone of the last poem of the sequence, "I Cry, Love! Love!" The poet's confidence here is not based on an exaggerated idea of his own importance or a delusion of complete self-knowledge, as lines like "Bless me and the maze I'm in!" (2.7) and "Behold, in the lout's eye, / Love" (2. 25–26) indicate. Neither is it based on mere "reason," as the opening of the poem's second section makes clear. Rather it is grounded in an expanded sense of self-acceptance which has developed over the course of the "tensed-up *Prelude.*" In "Open Letter" Roethke stresses the personal validity of the final vision of identity here:

> None the less, in spite of all the muck and welter, the dark, the *dreck* of these poems, I count myself among the happy poets. "I proclaim, once more, a condition of joy!" says the very last piece. (SP 40)

The line following this proclamation, "Walk into the wind, willie!" (2. 16), prepares us for the confident confrontation with death that occurs in the last section of the poem:

> I hear the owls, the soft callers, coming down from the hemlocks.
> The bats weave in and out of the willows,
> Wing-crooked and sure,
> Downward and upward,
> Dipping and veering close to the motionless water.
>
> (3. 1–5)

The scene here, with its "bats," "owls," and "hemlocks," is even more evocative than the one at the conclusion of "Praise to the End!," and Karl Malkoff finds an "implicit acceptance of the death wish" at the end of "I Cry, Love! Love!"[20] However, viewing this poem in the context of the sequence it originally completed, we can see that "I Cry, Love! Love!" is not a recapitulation of "Praise to the End!" but the culmination of the poet's response to it; the death-wish of the solitary onanist is replaced by a new perspective which confidently reaches out toward union with another person. The landscape of death at the beginning of the section is converted into a scene which compounds birth and procreation:

> Who untied the tree? I remember now.
> We met in a nest. Before I lived.
> The dark hair sighed.
> We never enter
> Alone.
>
> (3. 15–19)

Though sex is seen as a symbolic return to the womb, this new "entrance" does not represent the end result of a solitary man's wish for death but rather a union between two people which produces life.

In Part II of the final text, then, the isolated security of the "contained flower," at first countered by the onanism and death of "Praise to the End!," eventually grows into a "condition of joy" which points toward entrance into new life through sexual union. This vision is not reached directly by the adult mind of Part II but rather comes from a dramatic reliving of the poet's development from infancy to maturity. After this "tensed-up *Prelude*" has been written, the original ironic aspect of the title *Praise to the End!* is changed. The quotation from Wordsworth is no longer primarily a reference to the death-wish in a single poem but rather an allusion suggesting what the collection as a whole has accomplished: an inclusion of all the "terrors, pains, and early miseries" of past experience into a more accurate and secure sense of self-worth.

In the complex process of writing *Praise to the End!* Roethke proceeded, as he put it, "from exhaustion to exhaustion" (SP 39–40). Each apparent conclusion he reached— in the three-poem and later four-poem "Lost Son" sequences, in "Praise to the End!," and in the "tensed-up *Prelude*" that followed it—was incorporated in a broader cyclic pattern which then demanded new work as issues were raised through new juxtapositions of poems. Repeated plunges into "the dark world" of the past and the unconscious are at the heart of this process, gradually leading the poet toward deeper self-awareness. This work in cycles allowed Roethke to enrich and expand the process of self-discovery begun in the greenhouse poems, as he progressed from the careful examination of individual memories to an extended "history of the psyche" (SP 39).

CHAPTER FIVE

"Intuition" and "Craftsmanship":
The Poet at Work

You can take a dive in and you come up with all kinds of garbage
around your neck or you can bring up something beautiful.

It's the bringing together the whole thing into a coherent whole
that's hard for me. I mean that's the ultimate and the final work.
(TR 140–1)

In these comments from the interview for *In a Dark Time,* Theodore Roethke notes two major aspects in the composition of a poem:
the unpredictable "dive" into unconscious personal material and the
work involved in making the results of the plunge "coherent." We
have seen how Roethke gradually developed a coherent vision of self
through the cyclic process of composing and arranging the sequences
of his middle period. In this chapter I want to look at the process of
writing on a smaller scale, focussing on the poet's movement toward
self-understanding as he writes lines, culls them from his notebooks,
revises them, and arranges them into a finished work. The poems
included in Roethke's sequences of the '40s are extremely complex,
and this complexity is reflected in the writing process. Allan Seager's
estimate that only three per cent of what Roethke wrote actually
became part of a published poem[1] certainly applies to his work on
these sequences—the percentage of published work may, in fact, be
even lower. To avoid confusion in dealing with this intense and extensive process of composition, my focus will be primarily on the opening poem of *Praise to the End!,* "Where Knock Is Open Wide," but I
will also refer briefly to some of the other poems in the volume which
illuminate particular facets of Roethke's writing methods.

The framework I have found most useful for discussing the way

Roethke wrote the *Praise to the End!* poems is a three-stage compositional process. The first stage includes the generation of lines and scenes in fragmentary form in the notebooks. Roethke would periodically re-read and comment on what he had written in the notebooks, and it is generally at this point that he selected lines for his poems. While the first stage involved extensive "diving" into the unconscious, the second-stage work of reviewing and culling lines from the notebooks can be seen as the beginning of the struggle for "coherence." The third stage of composition involves the arrangement of lines and passages selected from the notebooks. This work was generally not done in the notebooks themselves but on separate sheets of paper, which can be considered the actual draft material of the poem. Revision, cancellation of lines, and addition of new ones occurred in all three stages of composition. The three processes I have described cannot always be clearly delineated in the writing of a given work; Roethke's compositional method was not that schematic. They do, however, provide a basic framework for tracing a poem's evolution from notebook jottings to finished draft. This three-stage process of generation of material, followed by selection and arrangement of lines, is similar in broad outline to Roethke's work on the greenhouse poems and those in *Open House,* but the complexity and intensity of the *Praise to the End!* poems led to substantial differences, particularly in the first two stages of the writing process, as we will see.

Before I discuss the composition of "Where Knock Is Open Wide," it is important to consider the special nature of this poem. Here is the work in its final version:

1

A kitten can
Bite with his feet;
Papa and Mamma
Have more teeth.

Sit and play
Under the rocker
Until the cows
All have puppies.

His ears haven't time.
Sing me a sleep-song, please.
A real hurt is soft.

Once upon a tree
I came across a time,
It wasn't even as
A ghoulie in a dream.

There was a mooly man
Who had a rubber hat
The funnier than that,—
He kept it in a can.

What's the time, papa-seed?
Everything has been twice.
My father is a fish.

2

I sing a small sing,
My uncle's away,
He's gone for always,
I don't care either.

I know who's got him,
They'll jump on his belly,
He won't be an angel,
I don't care either.

I know her noise.
Her neck has kittens.
I'll make a hole for her.
In the fire.

Winkie will yellow I sang.
Her eyes went kissing away
It was and it wasn't her there
I sang I sang all day.

3

I know it's an owl. He's making it darker.
Eat where you're at. I'm not a mouse.
Some stones are still warm.
I like soft paws.
Maybe I'm lost,
Or asleep.

A worm has a mouth.
Who keeps me last?
Fish me out.
Please.

God, give me a near. I hear flowers.
A ghost can't whistle.
I know! I know!
Hello happy hands.

4

We went by the river.
Water birds went ching. Went ching.
Stepped in wet. Over stones.
One, his nose had a frog,
But he slipped out.

I was sad for a fish.
Don't hit him on the boat, I said.
Look at him puff. He's trying to talk.
Papa threw him back.

Bullheads have whiskers.
And they bite.

        He watered the roses.
        His thumb had a rainbow.
        The stems said, Thank you.

Dark came early.

That was before. I fell! I fell!
The worm has moved away.
My tears are tired.

Nowhere is out. I saw the cold.
Went to visit the wind. Where the birds die.
How high is have?
I'll be a bite. You be a wink.
Sing the snake to sleep.

5

Kisses come back,
I said to Papa;
He was all whitey bones
And skin like paper.

God's somewhere else,
I said to Mamma.
The evening came
A long long time.

I'm somebody else now.
Don't tell my hands.
Have I come to always? Not yet.
One father is enough.

Maybe God has a house.
But not here.

"Where Knock Is Open Wide" was conceived as the beginning poem
of a sequence tracing a child's development into adulthood, and as
such it presented Roethke with certain problems not found in the other
poems of the volume. In an early, untitled draft of what would eventually become *Praise to the End!*, "Where Knock Is Open Wide" is not
numbered with the other works but rather set apart and labeled "Prologue" (TR 26–7). As the prologue to Roethke's "tensed-up *Prelude*,"

the poem had to give the reader starting the volume a clear sense of the speaker of the sequence. In Wordsworth's *Prelude* this sense of an "I" is largely achieved through the device of a self-conscious adult narrator reminiscing about his childhood. Roethke, however, wanted a "tensed-up" version which would remove the element of remembrance and show the child's feelings dramatically. These feelings came to the poet from memory, of course, but Roethke's task was to keep the process of remembering—and the adult identity it implies—out of the poem, creating a prologue with "no comment; everything in the mind of the kid" (SL 148). In his essay "Open Letter" the poet further defined his task:

> I believe that, in this kind of poem, the poet, in order to be true to what is most universal in himself, should not rely on allusion; should not comment or employ many judgment words; should not meditate (or maunder). He must scorn being "mysterious" or loosely oracular, but be willing to face up to genuine mystery. His language must be compelling and immediate: he must create an actuality. He must be able to telescope image and symbol, if necessary, without relying on the obvious connectives: to speak in a kind of psychic shorthand when his protagonist is under great stress. He must be able to shift his rhythms rapidly, the "tension." He works intuitively, and the final form of his poem must be imaginatively right. (SP 42)

The result is writing that relies primarily on images and fragments of narrative to create the "actuality" of the child's psychological experience, to show us the boy's development as it occurs rather than commenting on it or judging it in the Wordsworthian manner. This "actuality," of course, goes beyond the merely literal. Language in the poem is made "compelling and immediate" by its simplicity and concreteness. Depleted of abstractions and "judgment words" and wrenched from standard patterns of organization, Roethke's "psychic shorthand" goes beyond everyday meanings to take on a broader range of significance through associations of images.

When I looked at the notebooks in which Roethke did most of his early work on *Praise to the End!*, I was struck by the frenetic, exhaustive nature of his attempt to get lines and scenes on the page. He does not write his memories and feelings out systematically; there are no outlines of events or sequences. Rather he begins with a line or phrase, adds more lines, or perhaps a prose comment, then drops them and goes on to another item. Although it is more fragmented, this work is basically similar to that in the notebooks of the early '40s. But the lengthy descriptive passages of "looking" which characterize the greenhouse notebooks have all but disappeared, and much of the material is not related to specific scenes or memories at all. There are pages of completely disconnected lines which seem to have surfaced "raw" from the unconscious, dripping with associations but having no clear literal meaning. Judging from handwriting, types of ink, and occasional dating, it is clear that these notebooks were written quite rapidly. The rapidity and lack of organization reflect the poet's interest in tapping the unconscious; this interest is based on a commitment to emotion and unconscious association—not concept, description, or memory—as the starting point for a poem. Roethke describes this process in the interview for *In a Dark Time:*

> ...the general genesis is: one begins with a mood of some sort...the mood may not always be related to the piece, or it may be. But...the actual writing.
>
> The genesis of it, I think, for me, usually takes the shape of a line, or one or two or three lines... and these lines may accrete, I mean, sort of gather similar lines and images, you know. (TR 140–1, Roethke's ellipses)

Plunging into the depths of the unconscious was not always easy, and Roethke occasionally resorted to some very straightforward, deliberate techniques in the process of defining his early character and feelings. Here is an example from the notebooks:

> I know three names.
> > Papa is Otto.
> > Mamma is Helen.
> > Uncle is Charlie.
>
> (TR 37–267)

This material is eventually rejected, perhaps because it is too stiff and simplistic. Though the language of the lines is child-like, they are much too schematic and rationally ordered to reflect a child's mind.

The presence of an adult consciousness arranging and essentially "forcing" this material through logic— an assertion, "I know three names," is followed by its proof—eliminates any possibility of what Roethke called "accretion" of lines and images through association. Another attempt at direct definition of past figures seems slightly more successful:

> Papa's a breath
> Papa's a nose
> He has whiskers
> Under
>
> (TR 37–267)

I keep wanting to finish this one—"Under his clothes?" "Under his toes?" In any case, this fragment is more vivid and concrete than the previous one. The bouncy, nursery-rhyme rhythms make the lines seem more spontaneous, less self-conscious than the earlier passage, and they push us toward completing the rhymed quatrain. I think they pushed Roethke too; he marked this passage for further consideration.

While the first entry is based largely on the repetition of a logical rhetorical construct, [character] is [name], the second is organized around repetition and variation in rhythm. The rhythmic change in the third line—the trochae-iamb line is replaced here by two trochaes— creates an expectation that the fourth line will return to the trochae-iamb rhythm. A rhyme with "nose" is also expected. This all may seem somewhat mechanical, but it is precisely the mechanical nature of the writing that frees the poet from the self-consciousness involved in a direct attempt to define himself. With the poet's focus shifted from self-definition to completing a quatrain, new aspects of his memories and feelings can surface without being immediately judged, modified, or arranged by the conscious mind. Though the difference between nursery rhymes and the spare forms of *Open House* is obvious, Roethke's use of repetition in sound to generate material for "Where Knock is Open Wide" does hearken back to his earlier work. In both cases conscious judgment is held in abeyance during the first stage of writing. The difference lies in what Roethke does once lines have been generated. In his work on the *Praise to the End!* poems there is no immediate drive to get beyond the aural level or form an ordered unit of meaning, as there is earlier. The rhythmic repetition in the later notebooks is not merely a device to create lines which can then be consciously arranged but a way of circumventing conscious meaning itself to develop something deeper. As Roethke wrote of Blake, "Rhythm gives us the very psychic energy of the speaker" (SP 79). It is psychic energy, the "actuality" of the child's way of thinking about Papa, that Roethke is seeking here.

Another common technique for generating material in the notebooks is the use of a nonsense line. Nonsense verse is a natural part of the child's world, and Roethke himself named Mother Goose as one of the "ancestors" of *Praise to the End!* (SP 41). One of the most noticeably nonsensical lines in "Where Knock Is Open Wide" is "Winkie will yellow I sang" (2. 13). Here are three notebook entries involving this line:

> Winkie will yellow, I sang
> And then, then fishes away,
> The school bell rang and it rang
> But I stayed I stayed all away

> Winkie will yellow, I sang.
> First time for pickles.
> I'll be double good. A whole bunch

> Winkie will yellow I sang sang sang
> Who needs our head. Swish. I'm myself

> (TR 37–267)

Each of these passages gathers new material in a different way. The first uses the nonsense line along with rhyme and meter to develop a quatrain about playing hooky. The fact that this is the longest and most successful of the three—its meter and rhyme on "away," as well as its intriguing use of repetition in the third and fourth lines, are seen in the final text (2. 13–16)—shows the importance Roethke places on aural effects as he writes. The second entry, like the first, arises from the bright emotional tone of the nonsense line, with the "singing" leading toward a brief narrative focussed on the boy's happy anticipation of eating pickles or seeing them made. In the third entry the nonsense line does not lead to a specific scene but is rather linked to a somewhat obscure statement about personal identity and identification of self with outside entities: Winkie and the child speaker appear to merge in the phrase "our head" and then separate at the end of the passage. Though the accretion here seems less successful than in the other two passages, the entry shows the primary value of nonsense lines: their flexibility in generating different kinds of new material. Lacking a specific meaning, the nonsense lines lead the poet to develop non-rational associations based on sound, emotional tone, and unconscious feelings. They provide a base for the accretion of new lines, without limiting these new lines to a particular subject or theme.

A similar device is used in the poems written from an adult perspective; but instead of nonsense, which would be inappropriate in these poems, Roethke uses particularly abstract or obscure lines. An example is the line "Is circularity such a shame?" (1. 8) from "I Cry, Love! Love!" By itself this line has only the vaguest meaning. Because of this indefinite quality, it is useful for the accretion of new lines, as in these notebook jottings:

Is circularity a shame?
To stand close to the heart of things
The coarse dirt glistening like salt
One cold rock

Is circularity a shame? A cat goes wider.
Wasps come when I ask for pigeons.
What beats in me I cannot bear.

(TR 37–104)

These two entries are typical of the accretion process in the writing of the adult poems. The first involves the exploration of a potential meaning in the obscure line; "circularity" means getting "close to the heart of things." In the second entry, the abstract line accumulates some concrete but equally obscure new lines. Unlike the new material of the first entry, these lines are not directly linked to the meaning of "circularity," but they are important in their own right and are eventually revised and included in "I Cry, Love! Love!" (1. 2) and "Give Way, Ye Gates" (4. 12–13). The latter inclusion, with "What beats in me I cannot bear" turning into its opposite, "What beats in me / I still bear," shows how little Roethke was concerned with the rational meaning of his lines during this first stage of writing. Generally, the composition of "Where Knock Is Open Wide" included fewer abstract lines of the "circularity" type, which would not fit the child's voice, and more brief verse narratives like the "pickles" or "playing hooky" scenes.

Nonsense, obscure lines, and nursery-rhyme forms all allow Roethke to generate unconscious material by circumventing judgment and interpretation. Story telling has a similar function. We have seen a rudimentary example of this in the "pickles" passage. Here is a more developed narrative entry:

> I'm fish. I'm father. Look, papa,
> Almost with the water.
> Tomorrow I'll be a
> Where's the fish?
> I've got a worm
> Darken last
> Dark's all night. Stand by a bush.
> Where's the fish?

$$(TR\ 37–267)$$

Like the "three names" and "Papa's a breath" passages, this entry begins as a fairly direct attempt to answer a question of identity: Who am I? It is reminiscent in this regard of Roethke's work on "On the Road to Woodlawn," which also began with direct, though somewhat more specific, questions. Though the opening lines focus on the central question, the last half of the passage moves away from this topic to set up a night scene that is eventually incorporated in Part 3 of the finished poem. The shift from self-definition to a kind of rudimentary story telling shows Roethke moving from a somewhat self-conscious level of writing—in which he approaches the challenge of self-characterization in this prologue poem directly—to a deeper, less conscious level— in which he dramatizes childhood experience, reliving it in words. Language in the narrative augments this movement. Primitive nouns like "fish," "water," and "worm" are, as Roethke put it, "drenched with human association" (SP 80).[2] They not only reflect a child's vocabulary but also allow access to deeper unconscious levels by means of these associations. At these deeper levels, the poet finds a way to progress easily from the memory of fishing with his father, which prompted his opening lines of self-definition, to the night scene. The key line here is the fifth; the phallic worm image links fishing with the child's awareness of his own body in bed. Though most of these lines do not appear in their original form in the published version of "Where Knock Is Open Wide," the linking device Roethke discovered in this entry is further developed in the course of writing and eventually serves to connect Parts 3 and 4:

> A worm has a mouth.
> Who keeps me last?
> Fish me out.
> Please.
>
> (3. 7–10)

While the notebook entry I have just examined moves from self-definition toward narrative, many passages in the notebooks move in the opposite direction. Here is a brief narrative Roethke considered for inclusion in "Where Knock Is Open Wide":

> I found a big worm for papa to fish with.
> Too big, he said. A garter worm.
> ~~Always something wrong.~~
>
> What's a worm you can't fish with?
> A Garter-worm. ~~Too big~~ No good, papa said.
> No good.
>
> Garter-worms you can't fish with.
> One I found by the well.
> He stuck his tongue out
> ~~Too big, Papa said.~~
> ~~He laughed.~~
> Too big, Papa said.
> I gave him back quick
> To the grass.
> Yes.
>
> (TR 37–267)

In the three attempts the poet makes at this scene, we can see his concern with the development of the story, not directly for self-definition, but for its own sake. The first version, for example, starts with a narrative statement in the past tense. By the second version the opening line has become a dramatic question, and in the third the whole point about garter worms is stated in one line. The basic memory at the core of the writing here is dramatized and condensed, so that by the third version it has become just the starting point of a more developed narrative. This process of accretion of new material through repetition and condensation of a memory is common in the notebooks.

As a little story is developed in this way, the poet's feelings about himself and the incident also develop. In this particular series of entries, Roethke moves from a direct expression of frustration and humiliation at offering the wrong kind of worm—"Always something wrong"—through a less emotional statement of fact—"No good, papa said"—to a final scene in which the worm is no longer "no good" but merely "Too big" and Papa is in a warm, "laughing" mood. The change in the poet's feelings suggests a new understanding of the memory involved here; the father's nurturing qualities have been rediscovered. Roethke gains this understanding not by concentrating on his emotions directly but by working on the dramatic narrative. This process involves turning a memory that had already been emotionally "judged" by the adult mind—"Always something wrong"—into a dramatic scene from the child's perspective. In this final scene, offering a garter snake instead of a worm is no longer an awkward blunder but rather a part of the learning experience which allows the child to state confidently, "Garter-worms you can't fish with"; the father, correspondingly, has changed from the boy's harsh critic to his loving guide. Narrative thus functions in a way similar to the non-sense, obscure lines, and nursery-rhyme patterns I mentioned earlier; it provides a structure that keeps the poet from focussing on large, conscious questions of identity— as he did in the unsuccessful "three names" passage—and helps bring unconscious feelings to the surface.

While the first stage of Roethke's writing involves techniques for freeing the unconscious as he generates lines and passages, the second stage— the selection and combination of fragments from the notebooks—relies more heavily on conscious decisions. I do not mean to suggest by this that Roethke completely understood or controlled all the material with which he was working at this stage. Like the writing in the notebooks, the selection stage was a process of discovery. But instead of discovering things indirectly through the act of writing about himself, the poet in the second stage has distanced himself somewhat from this writing and learns what the lines mean by seeing how they might work in the aesthetic and psychological contexts of a poem. Roethke's second-stage work on *Praise to the End!* is similar in broad outline to his work at this stage on the greenhouse poems; but, since the notebook material for the later poems is more frenetic and fragmented, the selection process involves more extensive work with smaller units, including individual lines or even parts of lines removed from their previous contexts. There is also a new element of time involved. The transition from the first to the second stage of composition hinges on a kind of waiting period between the generation of lines in the notebooks and their selection in a later re-reading. In that period the poet gains a clearer sense of what the potential poem might be— which is, of course, a considerably more difficult task for the complex *Praise to the End!* poems than for Roethke's earlier work. Roethke's comments on three poets he considered "intuitive" like himself— Stanley Kunitz, Jean Garrigue, and David Wagoner— describe this movement from the first to the second stage of writing:

> Usually they begin from within: the original impulse comes from the unconscious, from the "muse." They "wait"—and then subject the promptings of the intuition to the pressures of craftsmanship. They experiment, but usually within the tradition. With them, the poem, however oddly shaped or metrically rough, exists in itself, alive, an entity, complete and all of a piece. (SP 130)

For Roethke, the first step in subjecting his notebook jottings to "the pressures of craftsmanship" was a kind of winnowing process; the "chaff" generated in the first stage of composition had to be separated from the useful "wheat." As he read through the notebooks he had filled, Roethke would go over particular lines with crayon. What might seem at first like cross-outs in the notebooks are actually passages chosen for further consideration. In my quotations I have enclosed these selected passages in brackets. This entry shows the culling of lines on its most basic level:

> [What has the vine loosened? A lust for ripeness.]
> [Light comes in a dry day.]
> What have been your Sins? Or a
> [Mamma, put on your dark hood.]
> [It's a long way to somewhere else.]

Dead fly to the wind,
[A house for wisdom; a field for revelation]
Are flower & seed the same? Ask the ashes.

(TR 37–267)

This passage is a series of apparently unconnected lines, most likely
generated through the "obscure line" technique we saw in the various
"circularity" passages. It is clear that the poet did not have a particular
scene or even a general topic in mind when he wrote these lines.
Roethke's selections from the entry indicate an early phase of the second compositional stage, since here too there is little evidence that the
poet had an idea of a particular poem in mind; the chosen lines—
except for the second, which is not used—eventually surfaced in two
different poems, "Sensibility! O La!" and "Unfold! Unfold!"

What, then, did Roethke see in the selected lines? Why did he
choose them? It is hard to second-guess the poet here, but based on
Roethke's general poetic interests in this period, we can determine
several aspects that might have attracted him, including associational
richness in "light," "field," and "dark hood"; the musical effect of con-
sonance and repetition of long vowels in the first two lines; an element
of mystery in "somewhere else" and the difference between "house"
and "field"; the pun on "way" at the end of the second line; the ques-
tion-and-answer rhetoric of the first line; and the balance of the last.
Since the poet has no clear sense of overall concepts he wants
to develop at this point, any element—aural, rhetorical, or associational—in which Roethke detected "energy" could provide the basis
for selecting a line. In a panel discussion on Roethke's teaching, two
of his former students, Tess Gallagher and Jenijoy La Belle, noted
how this sense of the strong line apart from its context—what Roethke
called "the single phrase of real poetry, the line that has energy"
(SP 46)—informed his classroom work.[3] It also became increasingly
important in his writing, especially in the love poems of the '50s, as
we will see in the next chapter.

But the energy of single lines is not the only basis for their selection here. Though Roethke did not have a particular poem in mind
when he chose these lines, we can see a sense of order starting to take
shape in the pair of lines Roethke selects from the middle of the
passage, "Mamma, put on your dark hood" and "It's a long way to
somewhere else." The poet is perceiving a link between two lines

which were generated in a group of disconnected fragments. In their final version in "Sensibility! O La!," the two lines are joined by a semicolon and play an important role as the start of the movement toward affirmation—"I insist! / I am." (3. 24–25)—which concludes the poem. The selection process allows the poet to lift these two lines out of their original context, revealing the beginnings of a pattern that was not apparent during the first stage of composition. The discovery of connections of this sort is a vital part of the second stage of writing, particularly in the adult poems, for which much of the notebook material is made up of disconnected obscure lines.

Selection was not always made on a line-by-line basis. For example, Roethke crayoned over the entire entry describing the "garter worm" scene, with the exception of the last two lines of the second version. Since this entry includes three different versions of the same memory, it is clear that the poet was interested not in choosing individual lines here but rather in choosing scenes. The selection of a scene does not mean that it will be accepted or rejected as a unit in the finished poem. Though the "garter worm" passage is marked for consideration, none of it survives directly in the final text. There is, however, a fishing scene in "Where Knock Is Open Wide," as well as references to worms. What happens to the "garter worm" scene here is fairly common in Roethke's work with narratives in the notebooks. A passage is not "mined" for useful lines or considered as a unit for the poem; instead, significant images, situations, or shades of emotion are picked out and inserted in different passages, some of which surface in the finished work. The "garter worm" with its "tongue," for example, is removed from the fishing scene and transformed in the process of composition into the line "A worm has a mouth" (3. 7) from the night scene. The emotional content implied in the notebook entry, which involves the boy's sense of wonder and some anxiety about the phallic quality of the snake— "He stuck his tongue out"— is toned down slightly in the final version but is not significantly altered. Narrative details, phrasing, and language in notebook passages are often not as important at this stage of composition as the feelings and associative images behind them.

Another example of Roethke's distillation of notebook work is his selection of material about his Uncle Charlie, who appears briefly in Part 2 of "Where Knock Is Open Wide." Here is some of Roethke's extensive work on this figure, with the lines he selected in brackets:

He's gone for always
He didn't like mamma
He ate all the nougats
We'd saved for dinner

[He stole some nice money]
[He ate all the nougats]
I saved for papa
He broke
He lost my

I know who's got him;
And his sticky fingers

He didn't like mamma
And I broke his window

He was mean to mamma;
He ate all the nougats;
I know who's got him:
[They'll jump on his belly.]

Don't lift me up. ~~I'll pee in his face.~~ I
          don't want to see him.
They won't make him an angel.
I know where he's going.
They'll pinch him good.

(TR 37–267)

The entry from which I have taken these passages is an example of
Roethke's first-stage composition at its most active; two pages are
filled with lines and fragments, stanzas all in the same rhythm,
repeated lines that generate new stanzas, and pieces of dramatic narrative. In writing this entry, Roethke poetically pulled out all the stops to
get his feelings about Uncle Charlie on the page, but in the second
stage of composition he selected only certain details. In addition to the
lines I have marked in the previous quotation, the poet only crayoned
over one passage here:

> I sing a small sing;
> My uncle's away:
> He's gone for always.
> I don't care either.

This stanza, plus the following one, are all that is left of the material by the time the poem is completed:

> I know who's got him,
> They'll jump on his belly,
> He won't be an angel,
> I don't care either.

(2. 5–8)

In selecting the eight lines that make up the passage in its final version from the two dozen or so in the notebook entry, Roethke made Uncle Charlie less specific as a character; his particular offenses against the boy and his family are left out, as are the child's direct interactions with him, such as breaking his window or wanting to urinate on his corpse. Also, Uncle Charlie's relation to Papa and Mamma is removed, so that in the published text the focus is entirely on the boy's feelings about his uncle. In the notebook, Roethke found himself not only trying to express his childhood hatred for his uncle but also attempting to explain and to some extent justify it by dwelling on the uncle's transgressions; this is seen most clearly in the second stanza of the group I quoted, particularly in the fragmentary "He broke" and "He lost my" at the end. The fact that tne poet selected the two opening lines of this list of "crimes" for further consideration shows how long this explanation for his own feelings remained important to him. But as the poem began to take shape, Roethke eventually saw that the justification for the child's feelings was unimportant in the "entity" of the poem and that too much information about Uncle Charlie would detract from the central child-parents relation here. The question of the child's reasons for his feelings, which Roethke answered for himself in the notebook, is dropped when the poet considers the dramatic expression of those feelings in a poem. It is not coincidental that one of the quatrains Roethke retains is the most linguistically inventive— "I sing a small sing"— and rhythmically lively of the notebook passage. It is, as "Open Letter" would have it, "imaginatively right" (SP 42). For a poet who believed that Blake's rhythms revealed his psychic energies, the merging of personal and aesthetic concerns in the selection process was natural.

The process of paring down memories, of removing superfluous details and explanations in order to reveal an emotional core that is both dramatic and "imaginatively right," is common in the second stage of composition. While the poet in his notebooks is interested in liberating conscious and unconscious emotions, in the selection process he is primarily concerned with ordering feelings into effective expression. This is not to say that Roethke always had a definite idea of what that expression was to be, that his self-discovery ended at the notebook stage of composition. Rather, the selection and condensation of memories into dramatic units in a poem was a process of self-understanding through art. To make this process work, the poet had to proceed largely intuitively at the second stage, trying to discover aesthetic and psychological patterns, rather than fabricating structures and fitting notebook material into them. This is the opposite of Roethke's practice in his earlier poems. Contrasting Roethke's work on *Open House* with that since *The Lost Son,* William Meredith describes the change this way:

> Instead of ordering experience, these poems attend on experience with the conviction that there is order in it. However imperfectly his eye might see it or his voice might articulate it— and he went on writing occasional shapeless lines and passages all his life— this *revealed* order was the only one Roethke served from this time on. [Meredith's emphasis][4]

The period between the first and second stages of composition is essential to Roethke's apprehension of "revealed order." This "wait" and the self-distancing from the material it creates allow implications in scenes and images to surface, new associations to arise from the evocatively primitive language, new connections among lines and passages to reveal themselves, and unconscious feelings to become more comprehensible. As this happens, the poem is gradually lifted from the welter of fragments in which it began and starts to become, as Roethke put it, "alive, an entity" (SP 130).

As an entity, the poem no longer is part of the poet's continuing work in the notebooks; Roethke's shift of material selected from the notebooks to separate sheets of paper is a sign that he has come to some sense of the poem's individual identity. Sometimes that sense is quite vague; among the poet's notes and drafts are single sheets which seem to have little connection to the particular poem at hand, as well as drafts of unfinished poems which end in total confusion. But once a poem has entered this third stage of composition, there is a noticeable difference in the type of work Roethke does on it. The emphasis at this stage is on conscious, deliberate work. As the lines chosen from the notebooks are now seen as part of a specific poem, aesthetic considerations become more important than earlier. Unlike the work in the notebooks, where lines are repeated infrequently, primarily in the hope of generating new lines, the third stage of composition involves considerable repetition, sometimes of whole passages. In the draft material for "I Cry, Love! Love!," for example, the opening of the poem's third section is repeated fifteen times (TR 20–37). As he repeats passages, the poet makes line-by-line revisions, deletes extraneous material, and sometimes adds a line or two. In addition to this revision of passages, Roethke works extensively with the order of passages in each section and the order of sections in the poem, searching for a structure that suits his material.

Like the other two stages, the third phase of composition is a process of discovery. But while in the earlier stages Roethke gained self-knowledge by first writing and then observing what he had written, on the draft level he learns about himself largely through experimentation with his words and the discoveries he has made from them. This experimentation is founded on the increased distance from the personal material the poet has achieved after the first two stages of writing. Ironically, it is primarily this distance which allows him to discover in the different passages an order that illuminates psychological developments in his own life. As Roethke put it in one notebook, "The return into the self can be made only when something more than the self is there" (TR 38–111). By the third stage of composition the poet has turned his original notebook jottings into "something more than the self" and is now ready to use them for a "return into the self" in the act of constructing the finished poem.

As Roethke was putting "Where Knock Is Open Wide" together, he would make brief notes for scenes as they occurred to him. Here are two examples:

Hello happy hands, Hello big smile. I could smell
You coming papa   Can I have a schluck too
Even my ears are all right then I won't
have a fever

Hello happy hands hello big smile I know it was
you papa you don't crack sticks when you walk

(TR 24–67)

In the first note, written in a kind of half-prose, half-verse style,
Roethke links the image of "happy hands" to the appearance of his
father and notes two specific memories for consideration: asking Papa
for a drink ("schluck" is Midwestern German slang), probably from
his beer bottle; and escaping or recovering from a childhood illness.
The second note, written directly beneath the first on the draft sheet,
retains the link between "happy hands" and the appearance of Papa,
who now, however, has the ghostly characteristic of not exerting
weight when he walks. Though nothing but the opening three words in
these notes is kept in the finished poem, the encounter with a ghostly
father eventually surfaces in the last section of the poem, where Papa
is described as being "all whitey bones / And skin like paper" (5. 3–4),
and in the pivotal last stanza of Part 3:

God, give me a near. I hear flowers.
A ghost can't whistle.
I know! I know!
Hello happy hands.

(3. 11–14)

While "happy hands" in the two notes are clearly Papa's hands, going
along with his "big smile," in the final version of the poem they are
linked back to earlier images of masturbation in this section: "Some
stones are still warm. / I like soft paws." (3. 3–4); "A worm has a
mouth" (3. 7). With this link, the appearance of the ghost completes
the familiar equation, "onanism equals death," that Roethke had
developed earlier in "Praise to the End!" In the composition of "Where
Knock Is Open Wide," this point is not merely transferred from the
earlier poem and stated directly but essentially rediscovered in its new

childhood context through the process of bringing lines from the notebooks together with material generated in a kind of rambling commentary on the draft sheets. This commentary is not used primarily as draft material for the poem but functions rather as a catalyst to develop connections between images, clarifying the suggestions in different lines to set up larger associational structures within the poem.

The development of these larger structures is completed by Roethke's final and most extensive work at this stage in the writing process: the ordering of passages in the poem. In this process of arrangement, the poet is working at his most conscious level, focussing on the overall movement of the poem and the kinds of meaning the piece is to present. The clearest example of this work in the composition of "Where Knock Is Open Wide" is in Part 4. Here is an early draft of the section:

> Down by the river, water was watching.
> Birds stepped over the stones.
> One, his nose had a fish.
>
> Went to visit the wind. Where the birds die.
> I held my ear to a pole.
> The wood went hum.
>
> Papa watered the roses.
> He had a rainbow on his thumb.
> The stems said, Thank you.
> The light came early.
> Rocked the blossoms.
>
> (TR 24–67)

The draft from which I quote this passage is a skeletal version of the finished poem. The major work on the individual stanzas has been completed, and they are grouped in the five sections of the poem; but the order of the stanzas within the sections is still not fixed, and many passages have not yet been included. The central fishing scene in Part 4—the only extended encounter between the boy and his father in the poem—as well as several lines near the end of the section, are not in the draft. This early version of Part 4 is based on a simple dichotomy. In the first two stanzas the boy is alone in a rather hostile landscape

where birds snare fish and then die in the wind, water ominously
"watches," and the only communication with "nature" is through the
"hum" of a telephone pole. In the third stanza, the natural world is
benign; light comes to take care of the blossoms, and the plants thank
the nurturing father. A greatly idealized Papa is presented as a model
of harmony between man and nature.

This idealized vision, in addition to being rather simplistic struc-
turally, tends to gloss over the difficulties in the relation between
father and son. Though the simple dichotomy seemed appropriate to
Roethke in his early draft of the section, the other side of his feelings,
his sense of Papa as "Father Fear," was being left out. In his work with
memories of fishing at earlier stages of composition, Roethke had
developed a passage which captures his ambivalence about his father
dramatically through the associative language of the child. This passage was eventually added to Part 4 of "Where Knock Is Open Wide":

> I was sad for a fish.
> Don't hit him on the boat, I said.
> Look at him puff. He's trying to talk.
> Papa threw him back.
>
> Bullheads have whiskers.
> And they bite.
>
> (4. 6–11)

The father is not literally hurting the son here, but there is a violence in
his actions that arouses fear in the boy, who identifies himself with the
seemingly helpless fish. By the end of the passage, however, the
father is no longer seen as cruel—he throws the fish back—the fish is
no longer viewed as an extension of the boy or pitied; and the boy has
learned an important lesson from Papa, which he proudly states in the
last two lines. The image of the father as teacher and protector of the
son—from bullheads, and presumably other dangers—is shown as it
develops in the boy's eyes. Consequently, the scene of Papa watering
the roses in the stanza which now follows this passage becomes less an
artificial idealization for the sake of the dichotomous structure of the
section and more a genuine expression of the boy's love. The insertion
of the fishing scene gives us, and Roethke as well, a sense of *how* the
child learns to admire his father. It is the only scene in the poem in

which father and son are in close enough contact for this to occur. The added passage also unifies the associational structure of the poem as a whole by providing a central scene to augment earlier references to fish in the poem (1. 22; 3. 7–10). The fishing scene functions as a kind of vortex for what Blessing calls the "whirl of associations"[5] evoked by the important term "fish" in the child's primitive language.

With the new scene in the draft, the two-part emotional structure of Part 4 is altered, and a number of revisions and rearrangements of lines become necessary.

> We went by the river.
> Water birds went ching. Went ching.
> Stepped in wet. Over stones.
> One, his nose had a frog,
> But he slipped out.
>
> (4. 1–5)

In the first stanza, for example, the general scene is kept largely intact, but the disquieting image of the "watching" water is removed. Also, the bird no longer kills its prey; rather, the frog "slips out," setting up a parallel to the father's throwing the fish back. Perhaps the switch from a fish to a frog in the fourth line is a way of keeping the parallel from becoming heavy-handed. In any case, nature is made less threatening in the first stanza; nothing gets eaten. The boy's frightening visit to "the wind. Where the birds die" is now placed after the fishing and greenhouse scenes, in the two rather bleak stanzas which conclude the section:

> That was before. I fell! I fell!
> The worm has moved away.
> My tears are tired.
>
> Nowhere is out. I saw the cold.
> Went to visit the wind. Where the birds die.
> How high is have?
> I'll be a bite. You be a wink.
> Sing the snake to sleep.
>
> (4. 16–23)

These stanzas appear in the final version as an emotional counter to the idealized vision of Papa in the greenhouse and help prepare the reader for the boy's grim encounter with the ghost father in Part 5 after the "fall." The conclusion of "Where Knock Is Open Wide" is bleak, but the revised fishing scene in Part 4 now provides a model for the boy's later development. The first successful encounter between father and son, it becomes an important touchstone in the sequence as a whole. Revision of other parts of a poem after the insertion of a new passage like the fishing scene is frequent in the third stage of composition; in it we can see Roethke consciously adjusting the movement of his poem to take into account the new understanding he has gained in the course of arranging his material.

Writing was never a simple process for Roethke. The composition of "Where Knock Is Open Wide" and other poems in *Praise to the End!* involved the liberation of unconscious material through rapid, often irrational writing in the notebooks; periods of waiting; selection of lines and passages from the notebooks; revision, addition, and deletion of lines; and experimentation with the order of scenes. At each stage the poet made new discoveries. Early formulations of memories and emotions were continually reviewed from new perspectives in a version of the cyclic method Roethke used in arranging the sequences. The result was an ever more inclusive vision of self, rooted in a dramatic reliving of the past. In essence, Roethke learned what he had to say about himself in the process of saying it. But though the poet placed great stress on intuition and the unconscious in the process of self-discovery through writing, the scenes and feelings in the finished volume, and the vision of self they comprise, did not arise spontaneously. As the poet James Wright, a friend and former student of Roethke, put it:

> He understood that the relation between the craft and the mysterious imagination is not what we conventionally think it to be. There are some people who think that a very careful, conscious craftsmanship will repress your feelings. And Roethke understood that it is careful, conscious craft which liberates your feelings and liberates your imagination.[6]

By subjecting "the promptings of the intuition to the pressures of craftsmanship" (SP 130), Roethke came to understand what his past and feelings meant.

CHAPTER SIX

"In Another Being, at Last":
Roethke's Love Poems

The publication of *Praise to the End!* in November, 1951 marks the end of Theodore Roethke's most experimental period. In an application for a Ford Foundation grant in early 1952, the poet referred to "new poems of a more formal order" and stated, "In poetry, I have exploited the personal myth as far as I wish to at the present time.... I am confident that I shall break into an entirely different style as a writer" (SL 173). Roethke received the grant, and his prediction turned out to be largely correct. The two aspects Roethke notes here— a movement away from "the personal myth" and a movement toward more formal verse—come together in the love poems of the poet's last three volumes. In this chapter I want to discuss Roethke's progress beyond the exclusively personal through his development of the love poem. This development in Roethke's career, like most, has its origins in the notebooks. After examining the basic changes in the notebook work of the 1950s, we will consider the composition of three love poems of this period—"The Vigil" from the "Four for Sir John Davies" sequence in *The Waking* and "I Knew a Woman" and "The Dream" from *Words for the Wind*—and the relation of this work to what Roethke called his "metaphysical" poems. The last part of the chapter will be focussed on the love poems in Roethke's last book, *The Far Field,* published in 1963. Fundamentally different from the poems of the '50s, these represent the culmination of Roethke's work with the love lyric in his movement beyond "the personal myth."

Writing to Marguerite Caetani in 1957, Roethke expressed his wish to have *Words for the Wind* published as a collection of new poems only, instead of a new-and-selected volume. Since Roethke's previous collection, *The Waking,* had included a selection of older work when it appeared in 1953, he naturally had doubts about repeating the format just four years later. But Roethke was less worried about the danger of publishing two volumes of new and selected work in a row than he was about his new work not getting proper attention. He wanted to "have Doubleday pump up old Theodore as a Love Poet, it being my *fiftieth* birthday on May 25, 1958, damn it all!" (TR 149–14, Roethke's emphasis). Though the poet was overruled by his editor on the contents of *Words for the Wind,* Roethke's comment shows how important the new love poems were to him at this stage in his career. He was self-conscious about his age—he had married only five years earlier and once jokingly compared himself to Yeats who "collapsed into matrimony around 50" (SL 179)—and he felt, rightly, that the love poems were a significant departure from anything he had done previously. As Coburn Freer notes in "Theodore Roethke's Love Poetry," there are no real love poems in Roethke's first three books and the few pieces that refer to adult sexual relations in these volumes are characterized by a "complete detachment" from the experience.[1]

Genuine love, of course, would have run counter to the tough sense of identity Roethke created in *Open House,* and the poet's concern in his next two volumes with *self*-discovery precluded any extensive treatment of adult personal relations. The adult poems in *Praise to the End!* are not about love itself but rather the psychic and spiritual struggles the poet must undergo *before* he is able to love. The immersion in memory, the unconscious, and self-reflection Roethke undertook in the 1940s, rewarding as it was, could only carry him so far. Stanley Kunitz sensed the limitations in this subject and method as early as 1949 in his review of *The Lost Son:* "It would seem that Roethke has reached the limits of exploration in this direction, that the next step beyond must be either silence or gibberish."[2] Kunitz, of course, could not foresee the role of *Praise to the End!* in developing the poet's exploration of self from infancy to adulthood, but his remark points to the dangers of an increasing solipsism, in which the poet ends up speaking only to himself, or not at all. Stephen Spender describes the next step in the poet's development this way:

> But there inevitably is a stage when he becomes aware of the split between the "I" and "the other." Then it becomes a matter of life and death for him to bridge the gulf between insideness and outsideness.

> The means by which the gulf is to be bridged is, of course, love; and
> "the other" who can release him from his imprisonment in the self is
> a woman.[3]

Roethke's awareness of the gap between self and other comes only
after he has traced the development of his identity in *Praise to the End!*
What had been a rich area for exploration, defined now by the printed
text, becomes a small world whose limitations are apparent. With no
significant relations outside this world, the poet finds himself "impris-
oned." Roethke's love poems are part of the general drive to escape
self-isolation which is a central feature of the last part of his career.

Roethke's sense of the limitations of the self as a subject coincide
with an increasing frustration about the type of poem he was writing.
This frustration is apparent in "O, Thou Opening, O," a poem in the
old "psychic shorthand" written after the completion of *Praise to the
End!* This awkwardly self-conscious poem, in which Roethke makes
announcements like "I'll change the image" (1. 19) or "Let me persuade more slowly" (2. 11), collapses into self-rebuking prose in its
middle section:

> And now are we to have that pelludious Jesus-shimmer over all
> things, the animal's candid gaze, a shade less than feathers, light's
> broken speech revived, a ghostly going of tame bears, a bright moon
> on gleaming skin, a thing you cannot say to whisper and equal a
> Wound?
> I'm tired of all that, Bag-Foot. I can hear small angels anytime.
> Who cares about the dance of dead underwear, or the sad waltz of
> paper bags? Who ever said God sang in your fat shape? You're not
> the only keeper of hay. That's a spratling's prattle. And don't be
> thinking you're simplicity's sweet thing, either. A leaf could drag
> you. (2. 1–9)

Ecstatic union with nature, the return to innocence, the poet's sense of
himself as a visionary— all the trademarks of the *Praise to the End!*
poems are now seen as "prattle" by a man who is "tired of all that." To
escape the "prison" of self, Roethke had to write an entirely different
kind of poem.

It may seem surprising that this movement beyond the limitations
of the self should be coupled with a return to formal verse. We have

seen how form in *Open House* helped Roethke build a defensive, closed sense of identity. But form can also serve as a bridge out of isolation. Roethke's story of the origin of "The Dance" from "Four for Sir John Davies" is illuminating here:

> I was in that particular hell of the poet: a longish dry period. It was 1952, I was 44, and I thought I was done. I was living alone in a biggish house in Edmonds, Washington. I had been reading—and re-reading—not Yeats, but Ralegh and Sir John Davies. I had been teaching the five-beat line for weeks—I knew quite a bit about it, but write it myself?—*no*: so I felt myself a fraud.
>
> Suddenly, in the early evening, the poem "The Dance" started, and finished itself in a very short time—say thirty minutes, maybe in the greater part of an hour, it was all done. I felt, I *knew,* I had hit it. I walked around, and I wept; and I knelt down—I always do after I've written what I know is a good piece. But at the same time I had, as God is my witness, the actual sense of a Presence—as if Yeats himself were *in* that room. The experience was in a way terrifying, for it lasted at least half an hour. That house, I repeat, was charged with a psychic presence: the very walls seemed to shimmer. I wept for joy. At last I was somebody again. He, they—the poets dead—were with me. (SP 23–24, Roethke's emphasis)

Roethke's relief in completing this formal poem so quickly is at least partly a response to the change from the slow and difficult experimental work of *Praise to the End!* But the most significant aspect of his comment is not the apparent ease of writing but the attitude toward literary ancestors. The young poet who wrote *Open House* was obsessed with the eradication of any trace of literary influence, but by the early '50s Roethke found the "presence" of Yeats a salvation; instead of violating his carefully constructed sense of identity as it might have done earlier, it affirmed his role in the "community" of poets, freeing him from isolation. Critics have not always looked favorably on the connection outside the self Roethke affirms here—Thom Gunn called Yeats' influence "pernicious"[4]—but Yeats' "psychic" approval was necessary for Roethke to prove to himself that he was not a "fraud." Roethke's work in the five-stress line of "the poets dead" and his acknowledgment of the tradition in both the title of the sequence and the body of the first poem—"I take this cadence from a man named

Yeats" ("The Dance," 19)— reflects a desire to go beyond the self which is fundamentally different from his defensive assertion of identity in *Open House*.

This change in attitude toward literary ancestors has some intriguing ramifications. We have seen how the poet's need to "subdue the dead" in "Feud" and other early poems reflects a struggle with literal as well as literary ancestors. In *Praise to the End!* Roethke came to terms with his dead father, and I would suggest that this resolution affected his attitude toward poetic "fathers" as well. The idea that dead figures of authority are not necessarily destructive but can help the living surfaces near the end of the "tensed-up *Prelude*" in "Unfold! Unfold!":

> In their harsh thickets
> The dead thrash.
> They help.
>
> (5. 21–23)

The support of literary "fathers," according to Roethke, enables the poet "to be more himself—or more than himself" (SP 69). Yeats and Roethke's dead father in his benign aspect both give the poet a sense of "being somebody" again. In both cases, too, their aid is in response to the poet's feelings of isolation and worthlessness. In his comments on writing "The Dance" Roethke describes himself as "living alone in a biggish house" and feeling "done," "a fraud"; his elation after completing the poem is based on the fact that someone is now "with" him. As Jenijoy La Belle points out, Roethke's responses to literary ancestors were intertwined with his feelings about love.[5] Thus it is not surprising that the poem which comes out of the poet's loneliness is not only an homage to Yeats and earlier masters but also the opening of Roethke's first sequence of love poems, "Four for Sir John Davies." The music of "the poets dead" lies behind the lines here, but it is "other wanton beats" ("The Dance," 21) that are the main subject of the sequence.

The way Roethke went about writing "Four for Sir John Davies" and the other love poems of the 1950s includes a few techniques developed from his methods of the previous decade. His early work in the notebooks, for instance, resembles the extensive "looking" at a subject found in the greenhouse notebooks; and, like the greenhouse poems, the love poems share a common origin in undifferentiated material. The major difference between the notebook work of the '40s and the early work on these love poems is Roethke's use of a metered line—iambic pentameter and, somewhat later, iambic trimeter—from the onset of the writing process. This difference corresponds to the change in focus from the self and memories—"the personal myth," as Roethke put it— to love. As the metered line alleviated Roethke's sense of poetic isolation by affirming his connection to "the poets dead," it also helped him get beyond the bounds of the isolated self in his subject matter.

Roethke's friend and former student, the poet Richard Hugo notes that when Roethke "felt himself going dry"—as he did in 1952—he always returned to form. Hugo's idea that "there is some correspondence of the form to psychic rhythms in the poet"[6] echoes his teacher's own concept of rhythm (SP 79) and is certainly true in Roethke's case: With the exception of two dramatic monologues in *The Far Field,* "Her Longing" and "Her Time," all of Roethke's love poems are written in meter, and almost all have rhyme schemes. There are, of course, important differences among the forms Roethke used, but it is clear that the movement outward from the self toward connection with another is bound up with the poet's return to form. While Roethke's work in free verse in the 1940s allowed him to range broadly through his past, learning what it meant as he imaginatively relived it, the movement back toward form in the 1950s signals his engagement with a new order of experience. The process of writing is no longer one of understanding what happened in the past but rather of discovering immediate feelings. Formal techniques, as we have seen, can help in this discovery by shifting the poet's attention away from the challenge of defining emotions, toward technical matters. As Roethke works to make the lines formally effective, his true feelings are expressed almost inadvertently. As Hugo puts it, the poet writing within formal constraints "is free to say what he never expected and always wanted to say."[7]

In his essay "The Teaching Poet," published in 1952, Roethke endorses Auden's metaphor of form as "a sieve…for catching certain kinds of material" (SP 48).[8] In the undifferentiated notebook work of the early '50s we can see the poet using the iambic pentameter line to gather the images central to his feelings about love. Music and the dance, the dream, transcendent ecstasy, animals, wind, water, and other prominent images in the love poems of the '50s crop up not only in material selected for the published texts but also in unused lines. Here are some examples:

The dances of the gander and the goose

(TR 39–126)

The denser things come close as if to kiss

(TR 39–124)

The flesh flies out beyond the windy void

(TR 39–126)

The doe leaps lightly through the windless wood

(TR 39–125)

An angel leaping high, foam-lovely bird

(TR 38–120)

It is tempting to second-guess the poet here: The "gander" and "goose," of course, belong in "I Knew a Woman"; "denser things" might fit "She"; the "flesh" line could be somewhere in "The Wraith" or "The Vigil" from "Four for Sir John Davies"; the "doe" could be in "The Dream," the "bird-angel" maybe in "The Swan" or "The Renewal." If we worked hard, we might be able to pinpoint the stanzas where the lines fit best. Or, we might build a new stanza from the unused lines. Each one has its own alliterative music; the images seem to complement each other; and there is even the possibility of a loose rhyme scheme in "goose" and "kiss," "wood" and "void." The fact that we—and Roethke—could do all this with lines composed completely independently shows the extraordinary flexibility of Roethke's work in the notebooks.

This flexibility is essential to the composition of the love poems. We have seen a similar quality in the obscure and nonsense lines of the *Praise to the End!* notebooks, which help the poet gain access to the irrational and unconscious parts of himself. But the lines in the notebooks of the '50s generally make sense; their flexibility stems not primarily from irrationality but from the fact that as end-stopped, metrical units sharing a common set of images, they are largely *interchangeable*. Their usefulness is not so much in the accretion of new material— judging from the notebooks, Roethke had little trouble spinning out iambic pentameter— as in the juxtapositions they can create when grouped in different ways. It is largely through these juxtapositions that the poet discovers what he feels. Since few lines in the notebooks contain clear statements of feeling in themselves, emotions must be defined by the interactions among images, and these interactions change as lines are grouped differently. In one notebook, for example, we find a couplet made up of one line that will appear in "I Knew a Woman" (23) and another from "The Wraith" (24): "A martyr to a motion not my own, / Impaled on light, and whirling slowly down" (TR 39–126). Though "I Knew a Woman" has a great deal of humor in it, the "martyr" line is not intrinsically funny; in the context of this couplet, in fact, it seems rather bleak. The couplet shows the poet considering the more literal qualities of the "martyr" image, such as transfixion, before he discovers the witty sexual innuendo of "motion" which will become clear when the line is included in "I Knew a Woman."

Returning to the five unused lines, we could start a love poem with this couplet—

An angel leaping high, foam-lovely bird,
The flesh flies out beyond the windy void—

or this one:

The denser things come close as if to kiss;
The flesh flies out beyond the windy void.

Despite the fact that the second line is the same in each example, two different ideas are developed here. The first pair stresses the transcendent divinity within physical love; the body becomes angelic. The second shows the body not in transcendence through love but in flight from the gross qualities of earthly passion. Because almost all the metrical lines in Roethke's notebooks of this period are end-stopped, this kind of experimentation with different combinations, and subsequently different expressions of feeling, comes easily. All I had to do in constructing the two couplets from Roethke's unused lines was insert either a comma or a semicolon after the first line. The comma added to the first couplet creates an apposition: The flesh is the angel.

But the semicolon in the second marks a less defined relation between the two lines; they stand in a kind of bare juxtaposition, in which the images interact based on their connotations and the context in which they are placed. In this example the semicolon suggests a temporal and causal relation: When the "denser things" near each other, flesh flies away. But this mark can also indicate parallel actions—

> The doe leaps lightly through the windless wood;
> The flesh flies out beyond the windy void—

opposition—

> The doe leaps lightly through the windless wood;
> The denser things come close as if to kiss—

or many other relations. Depending on the lines it connects, the semicolon can approach the comma, the colon, the period or any number of conjunctions in its effect. As used by Roethke, it is the least restrictive mark of punctuation.

Given its range of possibilities, it is not surprising that Roethke relied heavily on the semicolon as a linking device in his love poems of the '50s. One third of the lines in "The Dream," for example, including half of those in the last stanza, end in semicolons; one fourth of the lines in "I Knew a Woman" and one fifth in "The Vigil," "The Wraith," and other poems have this mark at the end. If we add to this lines ending in periods, we find a high percentage of fairly disconnected lines in these poems. This reflects, of course, the lines' independent origins in the notebooks. It also affects the way the poems work, as Robert Conquest notes:

> ...[Roethke's] method, very often, is to make a poem out of a series of sentences each perfectly clear and meaningful in itself but not logically connected with its successors. Yet these little gnomic phrases, sometimes under beautiful rhythmic control, are often integrated well enough into the poem's general drift, especially when that is a simple one. This is the case particularly in his poems on sexual themes.[9]

The disconnected lines in the notebooks allow the flexibility Roethke found necessary in starting to venture outside the self, but they also present the challenge of "integration" into the "general drift" of a poem.

While style and imagery are similar in all the love poems of the '50s, focus, tone, and resolution—the "general drift"— differ from poem to poem. For example, "The Vigil," "The Dream," and "I Knew a Woman" all arise from the same body of work in the notebooks, but each takes the material in a different direction. "The Vigil" is the most metaphysical, examining the question of mortality and the relation between body and spirit in love; "The Dream" stresses the ethereal side of love; and "I Knew a Woman" expresses its bawdy side. As Roethke re-read his notebooks and chose material for poems, he began to distinguish these and other specific aspects of his feelings about love. But his work in defining these different approaches was not simple or straightforward. As we will see, these three poems began in Roethke's attempt to complete the "Four for Sir John Davies" sequence; "The Dream" and "I Knew a Woman" were built from lines— and corresponding feelings— that were "left over" after Roethke ended the sequence with "The Vigil."

Roethke's initial sorting of material from the notebooks into broad categories is the second stage of writing for the love poems. Like the work of the '40s, it includes the selection of single lines from different contexts: "Who rise from flesh to spirit know the fall" from "The Vigil" (23); "I swear she cast a shadow white as stone" from "I Knew a Woman" (25); and "In that last while, eternity's confine" from "The Dream" (4. 7), among others, are all taken from a notebook in this way (TR 38–120). But this stage in Roethke's composition of the love poems is also related to the development of stanzas, as we can see from his work on "The Vigil." By the time he came to write this poem Roethke had already determined the six-line *ababcc* stanza in the first poem of "Four for Sir John Davies," "The Dance," and wanted to use it for the other poems in the sequence. The same notebook from which the individual lines I mentioned are selected contains completed stanzas like this one:

Passion's enough to give a being shape;
Solid the earth, and solider the air:
Eye learns from eye; cold lip from sensual lip;
Light hardened on the circles where we were;

> Astonied our souls stared into the black
> And formless night and dared it answer back.

(TR 38–120)

The closing couplet here is the prototype for the ending of the third stanza of "The Vigil"— "We danced to shining; mocked before the black / And shapeless night that made no answer back" (17–18)—but the third and fourth lines of the opening quatrain end up in altered form in the first stanza of "The Dream" (4, 6) and the first two lines are discarded.

The way Roethke worked on this draft stanza arises naturally from its form. In the *ababcc* stanza the couplet separates easily from the quatrain, especially when there is little enjambment. This separation between quatrain and couplet was important to Roethke; in thirteen of the sixteen stanzas in "Four for Sir John Davies" the couplet is clearly set off from the quatrain by a period or a question mark. In most of the stanzas the quatrain serves as a kind of exposition or narration of material, while the couplet with its tight rhyme responds to what has come before by summarizing it, adding a concluding detail, or stepping back and drawing a general point from the experience. In the draft stanza, for example, the couplet marks the completion of the "hardening," shape-developing process in the quatrain through the contrast between the lovers' "Astonied" souls— the pun is significant—and the "formless night." The couplets are central to the entire sequence; they define the poems' issues—"Was I the servant of a sovereign wish, / Or ladle rattling in an empty dish?" ("The Partner," 5–6)— summarize the lovers' progress— "In the rich weather of a dappled wood / We played with dark and light as children should" ("The Wraith," 17–18)— and clarify Roethke's major points with aphoristic generalizations—"All lovers live by longing, and endure: / Summon a vision and declare it pure"; "Who rise from flesh to spirit know the fall: / The word outleaps the world, and light is all" ("The Vigil," 5–6, 23–24).

In composing the sequence, Roethke not only removed selected couplets from completed stanzas as we have seen but also worked on couplets by themselves. One notebook has several pages of such work, including the couplet from "The Wraith" quoted above and this one from the previous stanza: "The valley rocked beneath the granite hill: / Our souls looked forth and the great day stood still" (TR 39–

126). In essence, what the poet is doing with both these couplets is developing a summary of the action in a stanza before the stanza itself is completed. It may seem that Roethke is working backwards here, from summary to narration, generalization to specifics; his method is the reverse of what we experience as we read the finished texts. But a completed couplet is an important tool for dealing with the mass of disconnected lines in the notebooks. It gives the poet a kind of emotional "sieve" with which to go through the notebook material, a context which allows him to see possible suggestions lines might have in a stanza and to determine which lines might be appropriate. Roethke first develops the witty sexual connotations in "a motion not my own," for example, after several bawdy couplets have begun to set the emotional tone for what will become "I Knew a Woman" (TR 39–131). In the case of the couplets from "The Wraith" we see an even more complex process, in which the poet tries them out like hats on different quatrains, at one point considering each of them as an ending for the first stanza of the poem (TR 24–76). Though the couplets in "Four for Sir John Davies" are not as interchangeable as the individual lines, they allow different juxtapositions with the quatrains which help the poet define his feelings.

As in Roethke's work of the '40s, the final stage of composition for the love poems is generally marked by the poet's transfer of material from the notebooks to separate sheets of paper. Though Roethke has a particular poem in mind when he does this, the sorting process is by no means over. As I mentioned, "The Vigil," "I Knew a Woman," and "The Dream" have a common origin in the notebooks, and it is not until "The Vigil" is completed that the other two poems are clearly defined as entities. This early draft of "The Vigil," for example, contains the "Passion" stanza with its lines from "The Dream":

The Vigil

What was there for the soul to understand?
All lovers live by longing and endure.
Hermes the shepherd walked the barren sand,
Summoned a vision, and declared it pure.
It was no change of light, or changeling's trick:
The vision faded when his soul grew sick.

Dante attained the purgatorial hill;
Trembled at hidden virtue without flaw,
Shook with a mighty power beyond his will,—
Did Beatrice deny what Dante saw?
That lady charged him with a carnal wish,
Rose up in glory when he purged the flesh.

Passion's enough to give a being shape:
Solid the earth and solider the air.
Eye learns from eye; cold lip from sensual lip;
Light hardened on the water where we were.
Astonied, the soul stared into the black
And formless night, and dared it answer back.

The world is for the living. Who are they?
We dared the dark to reach the white and warm.
She was the wind when wind was in my way;
Alive at noon, I perished in her form.
Who rise from flesh to spirit know the fall;
The word outleaps the world, and light is all.

                                        (TR 24–48)

Here is the final text for comparison:

The Vigil

Dante attained the purgatorial hill,
Trembled at hidden virtue without flaw,
Shook with a mighty power beyond his will,—
Did Beatrice deny what Dante saw?
All lovers live by longing, and endure:
Summon a vision and declare it pure.

Though everything's astonishment at last,
Who leaps to heaven at a single bound?
The links were soft between us; still, we kissed;
We undid chaos to a curious sound:
The waves broke easy, cried to me in white;
Her look was morning in the dying light.

The visible obscures. But who knows when?
Things have their thought: they are the shards of me;
I thought that once, and thought comes round again;
Rapt, we leaned forth with what we could not see.
We danced to shining; mocked before the black
And shapeless night that made no answer back.

The world is for the living. Who are they?
We dared the dark to reach the white and warm.
She was the wind when wind was in my way;
Alive at noon, I perished in her form.
Who rise from flesh to spirit know the fall:
The word outleaps the world, and light is all.

"The Vigil" underwent major revisions. While the second and fourth
stanzas of the draft are kept largely intact, Roethke eliminates the first
and third stanzas, using only two lines from the first (2, 4) in a different context in the finished poem (5–6). The quatrain of the draft's second stanza is moved up to the beginning, and two new stanzas are
added to fill in the middle. It is not faults in individual lines that led to
these extensive changes; there is little evidence of poetic "tinkering"
inside the lines, and, as we have seen, Roethke uses some of the lines
in the discarded stanzas in both "The Vigil" itself and later in "The
Dream." Rather, the revisions reflect the poet's concern with the emotional progression of the poem. Roethke's sense that something was
wrong with the way the draft was moving is seen in his first attempts to
revise it, which are focussed on the couplets, the lines where the progress of the poem tends to be summarized: New couplets are added to
the second, third, and fourth stanzas (TR 24–48). The couplet added
to the third stanza is the one we see in the finished text, but the other
two did not survive in the final version.

The problems in the draft could not be solved by simple revision
of the couplets. Even with the new couplets Roethke considered, the
structure of the poem feels static, its conclusion unpersuasive. The
first and second stanzas of the draft essentially repeat the same point
about ideal visions having their origins in physical reality, and since
both stanzas are allusive and impersonal, the "I" and "she" who are
central to the sequence do not appear until the poem is half over. The

third stanza in the draft shows the lovers developing a "shape," a physical reality with which to confront the chaos of the "night" of death; this concept remains in the final version. But the draft stanza is flawed by its opening, "Passion's enough to give a being shape," which presents the central idea as a given, so that the rest of the stanza seems a mere illustration of a maxim instead of a series of events important in their own right. The point is just stated at the beginning rather than discovered as we move through the stanza, and thus it appears unearned. Indeed, with the draft's impersonal, repetitive beginning and the rather didactic third stanza, the vision of transcendence of mortality through physical love in the draft as a whole seems flimsy; despite its strengths, the last stanza is not well enough supported by the rest of the poem to prove its claims.

In his revisions, Roethke dealt with the problem of repetition and impersonality at the beginning of the poem by eliminating most of the first stanza. The finished poem still begins with a literary allusion, but the closing couplet of the first stanza—which the poet, thanks to his rhyme scheme and interchangeable lines, was able to "scavenge" from the second and fourth lines of the discarded stanza— now roots the "pure vision" in the experience of "lovers" rather than that of mystical shepherds. The new second stanza shifts the focus of the poem from "all lovers" to a specific "us" and sets up the central contrast between "chaos" and "kisses," death and love. In the revised third stanza we can now see *how* "Passion" creates a "shape" with which to confront the "night"; by coming back to the metaphor of the dance, Roethke not only clarifies the process here but also helps unify the "Four for Sir John Davies" sequence as a whole. The last stanza's confident assertion of the lovers' triumph over chaos, dark, and death now follows naturally. It feels authentic because the revised poem traces the emotional progression that led to this claim from the lovers' "pure vision," through the first "kisses" that strengthen the "soft links" and "undo" the "chaos," to the ecstatic "dance" of union which culminates in a sexual "dying" that affirms love's transcendence of death. In revising "The Vigil," Roethke brought repetitious and disconnected expressions of emotion into a logical progression, clarifying the development of his feelings as he arranged their final expression in the poem.

Though "The Vigil" makes an effective conclusion to "Four for Sir John Davies," Roethke did not always conceive of the poem as ending a four-part sequence. In a letter written in September, 1952, the poet noted that "The Dance," "The Partner," and "The Wraith" were the first three poems of a series and added, "I may do a few more" (TR 148–33). Here is a poem he considered for the group but eventually rejected:

The Mentor

How well her wishes went: she stroked my chin;
She taught me turn and counter-turn, and stand;
She taught me touch, that swart hilarious skin;
I nibbled meekly from her proffered hand.
She was the sickle; I, poor I, the rake,
Coming behind her for her pretty sake.

Love likes a gander, and adores a goose;
The small birds flew in circles where we stood;
We played it quick; we played it light and loose;
The doe stood staring in the windless wood;
Cloud piled on cloud in the empyreal blue;
The wind rose up, and we knew what to do.

Though everything's astonishment at last,
Who leaps to heaven at a single bound?
The links were soft between us; still, we kissed;
We undid chaos to a curious sound.
The waves broke easy, cried to me in white;
Her look was morning in the dying light.

The visible obscures. But who knows when?
Things have their thought: they are the shards of me;
I thought that once, and thought comes round again;
Rapt, we leaned forth with what we could not see.
We danced to shining; mocked before the black
And shapeless night that made no answer back.

(TR 20–38)

"The Mentor" is the clearest example of the way the composition of "Four for Sir John Davies" is bound up with that of other love poems, in this case "I Knew a Woman." In clarifying the emotional progression of "The Vigil" by making the lovers more explicit, Roethke did not go back to his notebooks for new material but rather turned to the most specifically erotic poem in the draft sequence, "The Mentor," where the "steps" of the "dance"— "turn," "counter-turn," and "stand"—are clearly sexual. Indeed, the first half of this poem, with its "rake" and "goose" puns and its reliance on verbs like "touch," "stroke," and "nibble," has a sly tone and physicality that have little in common with the metaphysical concerns of the sequence. Roethke, of course, was interested in the second half of the poem, where "The Mentor" shifts its focus abruptly to the lovers' triumph over death, and the tone changes from the risqué wit of the punster to the more speculative, philosophical voice of a man interested in the deeper significance of his experience. "The Mentor" is a mismatched pairing of two different approaches to love. Roethke's "raid" on it not only helped clarify "The Vigil" but also eliminated a simplistic attempt to progress from the physical to the metaphysical side of love.

Only after he had removed the last half of "The Mentor" and subsequently completed "The Vigil" and the "Four for Sir John Davies" sequence did Roethke perceive where the opening stanzas of "The Mentor" were headed. In building "I Knew a Woman" from the remaining first half of "The Mentor," Roethke developed a side of his feelings about love which could not be expressed in "Four for Sir John Davies." Here is the final result:

I Knew a Woman

I knew a woman, lovely in her bones,
When small birds sighed, she would sigh back at them;
Ah, when she moved, she moved more ways than one:
The shapes a bright container can contain!
Of her choice virtues only gods should speak,
Or English poets who grew up on Greek
(I'd have them sing in chorus, cheek to cheek).

How well her wishes went! She stroked my chin,
She taught me Turn, and Counter-turn, and Stand;
She taught me Touch, that undulant white skin;
I nibbled meekly from her proffered hand;
She was the sickle; I, poor I, the rake,
Coming behind her for her pretty sake
(But what prodigious mowing we did make).

Love likes a gander, and adores a goose:
Her full lips pursed, the errant note to seize;
She played it quick, she played it light and loose;
My eyes, they dazzled at her flowing knees;
Her several parts could keep a pure repose,
Or one hip quiver with a mobile nose
(She moved in circles, and those circles moved).

Let seed be grass, and grass turn into hay:
I'm martyr to a motion not my own;
What's freedom for? To know eternity.
I swear she cast a shadow white as stone.
But who would count eternity in days?
These old bones live to learn her wanton ways:
(I measure time by how a body sways).

In addition to bringing in a new first stanza which sets the tone of bawdy humor right away, Roethke replaces the less witty parts of "The Mentor" with material more in keeping with the new tone; from the second stanza of the draft he uses only the *a* lines from the original *abab* quatrain, keeping the "loose" "play" and the "gander" and the "goose" while replacing the non-erotic references to nature in the *b* lines and the couplet with new lines about "flowing knees," "hips," and "a mobile nose." He adds a concluding stanza which parodies metaphysical speculation, implying that for the lover questions of time and mortality are subsumed in the more pressing drive to "learn her wanton ways." But what really solidifies Roethke's new tone in "I Knew a Woman" is its form: The addition of an extra rhyming line at the end of the old six-line stanza completely changes the way the stanza works. While the couplet in the *ababcc* stanza of "Four for Sir John Davies" uses rhyme to summarize or clarify the stanza, three rhyming lines—especially when the rhymes are full, as all but one in "I Knew a Woman" are—draw too much attention to themselves to be effective in this way; and the parentheses around the last line make the triple rhyme even more obvious. The six-line stanza gives the effect of logical, step-by-step progress. But the seven-line stanza with a triplet on the end is funny; it goes too far somehow, beyond what is needed for clear argument. In "I Knew a Woman" this humorous "overload" of rhyme augments the delight in sensual abundance at the heart of the poem and Roethke's feelings.

If "I Knew a Woman" rejoices in the physicality of love, another poem which arises after the completion of "Four for Sir John Davies" and includes lines from both "The Mentor" and an early draft of "The Vigil" depicts the trance-like process of falling in love:

The Dream

1

I met her as a blossom on a stem
Before she ever breathed, and in that dream
The mind remembers from a deeper sleep:
Eye learned from eye, cold lip from sensual lip.
My dream divided on a point of fire;
Light hardened on the water where we were;
A bird sang low; the moonlight sifted in;
The water rippled, and she rippled on.

2

She came toward me in the flowing air,
A shape of change, encircled by its fire.
I watched her there, between me and the moon;
The bushes and the stones danced on and on;
I touched her shadow when the light delayed;
I turned my face away, and yet she stayed.
A bird sang from the center of a tree;
She loved the wind because the wind loved me.

3

Love is not love until love's vulnerable.
She slowed to sigh, in that long interval.
A small bird flew in circles where we stood;
The deer came down, out of the dappled wood.
All who remember, doubt. Who calls that strange?
I tossed a stone, and listened to its plunge.
She knew the grammar of least motion, she
Lent me one virtue, and I live thereby.

4
She held her body steady in the wind;
Our shadows met, and slowly swung around;
She turned the field into a glittering sea;
I played in flame and water like a boy
And I swayed out beyond the white seafoam;
Like a wet log, I sang within a flame.
In that last while, eternity's confine,
I came to love, I came into my own.

William J. Martz describes the "tonal contrast" between "I Knew a Woman" and "The Dream," noting that the "exaggerations" and "wit" of the former are "muted" in "The Dream" and that full rhyme has given way to slant rhyme.[10] The difference in stanzaic form is also significant here. While both "I Knew a Woman" and "Four for Sir John Davies" are based on stanzas that tend to separate into two units, the quatrain and the couplet or triplet, "The Dream" is a series of half-rhymed couplets, the effect of which is neither witty nor argumentative. The poet's interest here is not in setting up a linear progression of ideas, as in Pope, but rather in gathering a number of parallel elements among which more complex interactions can take place. The use of the same pattern for thirty-two lines has a dream-like effect; distinctions between experience and judgment, narration and summary are blurred, and feelings are not developed sequentially but rather through a gradual, cumulative process. Richard Blessing notes the repetition of words within lines which is central to this process, pointing out that one out of every four lines in "The Dream" repeats a word or phrase.[11]

Repetition between stanzas is also important. Images like fire, the moon, or wind come back again and again in the different stanzas, accumulating significance as they reappear in subtly changed contexts. This is another version of the technique of cyclic progress Roethke first developed in his work of the 1940s. The way the bird in the poem progresses from "singing low" in an undefined location in Stanza 1, to singing "from the center of a tree" in Stanza 2, to flying in circles next to the lovers in the third stanza is an example of this process on its simplest level. The repeating image augments the slow, cyclic movement toward love in the poem not because of its intrinsic meaning but because of the way it has gradually changed each time it comes back. Unlike the step-by-step approach of "The Vigil" or the

comic overload of "I Knew a Woman," the emotional progression of
"The Dream" is based on variation within repetition. The couplets
create a loose framework against which the changes in the repeating
cycles become apparent.

These cycles build to the affirmation at the end of the poem: "In
that last while, eternity's confine, / I came to love, I came into my
own." The dream-like progress emphasizes the fact that the poet's triumph at the end is based not on conquest or an act of will but on a kind
of emotional surrender: "Love is not love until love's vulnerable." In
its final version, "The Dream" traces the poet's gradual acceptance of
his own vulnerability in love, but an earlier draft ends with this stanza:

> It's when I come to *therefore* I am lost;
> Was she a body, or a body's ghost?
> It's no small knowledge where the small soul goes;
> I've learned to dance upon arthritic toes.
> I drink and read from midnight until dawn,
> And feel a flush of wisdom coming on.
> And now my wisdom's come: I've learned to laugh;
> That laughter is my passion's epitaph.
>
> (TR 19–15, Roethke's emphasis)

Roethke's title for this early draft, "The Change," corresponds to the
concluding stanza in which the speaker wakes up to find his "passion"
gone, his "wisdom" merely self-delusion, his dream-lover largely
illusory. The self-mockery in this ending, with its alcoholic "flush of
wisdom" and the "dance upon arthritic toes" has charm, but the tone of
the stanza hardly fits the rest of the poem; in fact, it negates everything
that has come before. The first line of the stanza is an admission of failure, both in love and the poem. If the poet is "lost" here, it is not the
dream of love that misleads him as much as the attempt to resolve the
meaning of the dream and the poem as a whole with a simple "there-
fore"; the experience is too open-ended and subtle for this. Unable to
clarify the experience logically, the poet backs away from it into self-
mockery, assuming a defensive pose. The guilt and self-doubt against
which Roethke struggled in his sequences of the '40s resurface in this
draft, complete with "ghost"; the humorous description of self-
consciousness destroying the poet's "passion" thinly disguises the
old despair. What Roethke lacks at this point is the confidence to trust

his own vision. In replacing this draft stanza with the one in the published text Roethke not only unifies the overall tone of the poem, as he did in his work on "I Knew a Woman," but also comes to accept the dream vision even though its reality cannot be proved. In this he is vulnerable to betrayal and disillusionment, but this willingness to risk suffering is a necessary part of love.

In looking at the development of "The Vigil," "I Knew a Woman," and "The Dream," we have seen how Roethke defined different aspects of his feelings as he sorted out poems from a mass of undifferentiated material in iambic pentameter. The emotional progress from a largely metaphysical interest in love in "The Vigil," through witty sensuality in "I Knew a Woman," to genuine vulnerability and acceptance of someone outside the self in "The Dream" gives a simplified but accurate picture of what occurs as Roethke writes the love poems as a whole. As different poems are completed, new areas of feeling become apparent in the material left out of the finished texts; these "leftovers" are combined with new lines from the notebooks and other drafts in a rich process of cross-fertilization. The interchangeability of lines is essential here, so it is not surprising that the five-stress poems are composed independently from those in the other dominant meter of *Words for the Wind,* iambic trimeter. Though many notebooks of the '50s contain work in both meter and free verse, only a handful have both trimeter and pentameter lines in them. Roethke's writing method is generally the same for both meters, but he was clearly aware of the differences between the three and five-stress line and the different kinds of poem these lines could develop.

In a comment for the anthology *Poet's Choice,* Roethke compared his use of trimeter in *Open House* to that in "Words for the Wind," noting that the three-stress lines in the later poem were "swifter," the rhythms "more complex."[12] The increased subtlety of rhythm reflects the change from the use of meter to control experience and create identity in *Open House* to its use as a means to explore new relations outside the self in the love poems. Though all the love poems of the '50s are explorations of this sort, Roethke's efforts with the three-stress line are somewhat more complex than those in iambic pentameter. The intricate rhyme schemes of "Words for the Wind," for example, ranging from *abababcc* in Part 1 to an *abcbdbc* pattern in Part 2, *abcdacb* in Part 3, and *abcdabcd* in Part 4, would sound fussy and over-elaborate if attempted in pentameter—that is, if the rhymes

were noticed at all; in stanzas like those of Parts 3 and 4, where each
rhyme is separated by at least two non-rhyming lines, the pattern
would most likely not be heard.

The three-stress line, in contrast, provides a faster movement that
allows these more subtle rhyme schemes to work. This increased complexity and swiftness is reflected in Roethke's notebook work in trimeter, which shows more extensive experimentation with different
juxtapositions than does his work in pentameter. Notebook 39–138,
for example, contains twenty-seven straight pages of experiments
with different groupings of lines, including lists of possible rhyme
words, extensive repetition of selected lines like "All things bring me
to love" ("Words for the Wind," 3. 21) in different contexts, and
intriguing combinations in various stanzaic forms. Though most of the
trimeter lines arise as separate entities like their five-stress counter-
parts, Roethke occasionally even carves three-stress lines out of
unsuccessful work in pentameter, as when he takes the first three feet
of "Passion's enough to give a being shape" for Part 2 of "Words for
the Wind" (2. 15). Despite these differences, the basic feelings
behind the work in trimeter and pentameter are the same:

> And I dance round and round,
> A fond and foolish man,
> And see and suffer myself
> In another being, at last.
>
> ("Words for the Wind," 4. 21–24)

Like "The Dream," "Words for the Wind" is a poem about the surrender of will in love, the vulnerability which leads to a richer sense of
identity in union with the lover. In his comment for *Poet's Choice,*
Roethke noted the origins of "Words for the Wind" in a time when
"I was able to move outside myself—for me sometimes a violent dis-
location—and express a joy in another, in others."[13]

Working in both pentameter and trimeter, Roethke could develop
a range of different approaches, from the clear logical progression of
"Four for Sir John Davies" to the more lyrical movement in poems like
"The Dream" or "Words for the Wind." As we have seen, the poet
sorts lines and passages into poems which develop different tones,
clarifying his emotions as the poems are completed. I have been looking at poems which trace the positive steps in Roethke's movement

outside the self, but it is important to remember that the affirmative vision in these poems does not arise independently of other feelings. In a letter to Robert Heilman in 1956, Roethke defined his two central themes as "love and death" and found his work with them "exhausting," noting "you can't fool around, or just be 'witty,' once you are playing for keeps" (SL 208). In "The Pure Fury" the poet captures the link between these two themes in the first line of the last stanza—"Dream of a woman, and a dream of death"—and several of the other love poems in *Words for the Wind*, including "Love's Progress," "The Surly One," and "Plaint," develop feelings of loss, anxiety, and sorrow.

A letter from Roethke's friend and former student Carolyn Kizer links this element of despair to "guilt and self-contempt" in the writing process itself:

> These feelings can be temporarily smoothed out in the act of writing. But they have a curious way of back-firing within the poem. You realize that in the fluid forward motion of a poem, there is a very strong undertow pulling in the opposite direction: that undertow is the self-contempt, pulling you back to the shore from which you came. But the strong poem swims against it; and this tension, which can be, and often is, expressed in terms of a philosophical dialectic, really expresses the psychic drama of a poem, and makes it endlessly exciting.... I think one really dominates self-contempt only in the act of writing. (TR 8–28)

Immersed in self-contempt, the poet in the darker poems does not have the confidence and trust to venture outside the self. In "Love's Progress" and "The Surly One" Roethke is paralyzed by "fear"; in "The Pure Fury" a defensive drive to understand and control experience leads to rage; and "Plaint" carries self-contempt to its final manifestation in a death-wish: "Death is a deeper sleep, / And I delight in sleep" (17–18). In composing the more affirmative love poems, Roethke largely eliminates the "undertow" of self-contempt as he completes the writing process; the finished poem represents both an aesthetic and an emotional achievement. We might see the darker poems as the "back-firing" Kizer mentions, or at least as a kind of "back*sliding*" into defensiveness, loneliness, and fear of love, the "shore" from which Roethke started. Yet in their places in the "Love Poems" section of *Words for the Wind* these poems help create the "tension" which expresses the "psychic drama" of the group as a whole. The battle between "forward motion" and "undertow" that goes on in the process of writing results in a broad range of emotional tones as the poet resolves different parts of the struggle in different ways.

Kizer's reference to personal conflicts being expressed "in terms of a philosophical dialectic" is also significant here. As John Crowe Ransom and Frederick J. Hoffman have noted, Roethke's concerns in the love poems led him directly to the metaphysical issues examined in works like "The Dying Man" and "Sequence, Sometimes Metaphysical" from *The Far Field*.[14] There are obvious stylistic similarities between the love poems in *Words for the Wind* and these more philosophical pieces; and love, though not the central subject, figures prominently in many of these poems. The close relation between the love poems and the metaphysical work is further demonstrated by Roethke's draft and notebook material. This early work on "His Words" from "The Dying Man," for example, is focussed not so much on death *per se* as on the poet as aging lover; it contains a line that will be used in altered form in "Words for the Wind"—"A fair thing grows more fair" (2. 22)—and a title which suggests a more personal origin for the poem than is apparent in the published text:

Song for Middle Age

What lover keeps his song?
The small winds swirl around;
A bird puts out its tongue;
The trees turn in the light:
What fair thing grows more fair?
A breath is but a breath
Who would be half possessed?
My soul's hung out to dry
Like a fresh-salted skin,
I doubt I'll use it again
My soul's hung out to dry
But the spirit's another thing:
Eternity is Now,
The spirit has learned to sing.

(TR 23–62)

The metaphysical speculations on death here which will become the heart of "His Words" were culled from three-stress lines considered for the love poems. Roethke's changing the title from one suggesting a more or less personal lyric to one announcing a dramatic monologue— "His Words"— signals the poet's awareness of the new direction in which the material was headed. Another line from "Song for Middle Age," "Who would be half possessed?," turns up in "Sequence, Sometimes Metaphysical" ("In Evening Air," 1. 3), and there are several other examples of material "crossing over" from the love poems of the '50s to the philosophical poems in *The Far Field*. The phrase "love's a faring-forth," for instance, became part of "The Motion" · (3. 1) only after it had been considered for both "Words for the Wind" (TR 39–138) and "The Dream" (TR 19–15).

Clearly the sorting of three and five-stress lines into different poems did not end with the publication of *Words for the Wind*. "Sequence, Sometimes Metaphysical" from *The Far Field* was composed like the earlier love poems— to some extent composed *from* them—and represents an extension of Roethke's thematic concerns of the '50s: The movement out of the self toward union with the lover expands toward union with God, and failure in this movement, as seen in the darker poems, is more and more clearly identified with madness and death. Roethke's description of the turning point in the metaphysical poem "In a Dark Time" echoes the way the love poems move:

> "A fallen man" (literally and symbolically), I return to the human task of climbing out of the pits of fear—and this is not an ambiguous word: fear, unlike anxiety, has a definite object; I am afraid of God until—and here the transition is very swift—"The mind enters itself." The mind has been outside itself, beyond itself, and now returns home to the domain of love.[15]

If we replace "God" here with "love," we see the familiar struggle against fear and self-doubt and the final realization that to "come to love," as Roethke noted in "The Dream," is to come into one's own. Roethke's investigation of spiritual love in "Sequence, Sometimes Metaphysical" is grounded in his earlier exploration of erotic love.[16]

Though the metaphysical poems in *The Far Field* show clear links to the work of the '50s, the group identified as "Love Poems" in Roethke's last volume has, on the whole, little to do with the love poems of *Words for the Wind*. In style and tone the poems are quite varied, including witty personal poems like "The Happy Three" and "Her Wrath"; two dramatic monologues in free verse, "Her Longing" and "Her Time," which are reminiscent of Roethke's previous work in *Meditations of an Old Woman;* several highly lyrical pieces, including "Song," "The Apparition," and "The Young Girl"; and only two poems that rely on the three-stress, largely end-stopped lines and jux-tapositions of images seen in *Words for the Wind:* "Light Listened" and "His Foreboding." Both "Light Listened" and "His Foreboding" have thematic as well as stylistic connections to the poems of the 1950s: The concluding lines of "His Foreboding" appear among work on "Words for the Wind" and "All the Earth, All the Air" in a note-book from the early '50s (TR 39–138), and the kissing "more than twice" that opens "Light Listened" comes out of Roethke's early work on "I Knew a Woman" (TR 20–38), a poem the first stanza of "Light Listened" obviously echoes. Linked to the work of the '50s, these two poems do not represent any significant development in Roethke's sense of the love poem.

But the short lyrics that open the "Love Poems" section are some-thing new, and it is here that Roethke's work with the love poem cul-minates. The most striking quality of this new work is its lyricism. Drafts of the first poem of the group, "The Young Girl," show that Roethke originally considered it as the opening of a sequence to be called "Young Girl's Songs" or "Six Love Songs" (TR 24–78), and the song-like quality of the lines is readily apparent:

The Young Girl

What can the spirit believe?—
It takes in the whole body;
I, on coming to love,
Make that my study.

We are one, and yet we are more,
I am told by those who know,—
At times content to be two.
Today I skipped on the shore,
My eyes neither here nor there,
My thin arms to and fro,

A bird my body,
My bird-blood ready.

"The Young Girl" has a three-stress meter, but the rhythms of the poem are considerably looser than those in the trimeter work of the '50s; the couplet that ends the poem is in two-stress lines, and the iambic pulse that animates the earlier work is weaker in this poem as the lines approach the varied rhythms of speech. The imagery of "The Young Girl" is more simple and general than that in the work of the '50s, and the poem is considerably shorter than almost any of the earlier love poems. The brevity, generality, and more speech-oriented rhythms of "The Young Girl" and the other five love "songs" that follow it in *The Far Field* correspond to the overall vision of these poems. If the love poems of *Words for the Wind* and the metaphysical poems of *The Far Field* that come out of them develop structures in which complex emotional problems—the desire for love struggling with self-contempt, union with another hindered by defensiveness—can be examined and resolved, the love "songs" replace examination with assertion, resolution of problems with direct expression of feelings. In "Theodore Roethke's Love Poetry," Coburn Freer notes that the speaker of these poems asserts from the very beginning of the group "an identity of body and spirit," is "at ease" with herself and nature, sees "unity everywhere," and "has moved beyond intellect and 'ideas,' to make a direct synthesis of thing and sensation."[17]

Seeing "serious limitations" in this lyrical, non-analytical work, Freer argues that the love "songs" involve "heightened yet generalized passion" and the speaker in them "does not show much concern for or interest in the consciousness of her lover." Though he exaggerates the speaker's lack of concern here—both "The Apparition" and "Her Reticence" are based on the girl's worries about her lover's feelings—Freer's observations are basically correct. But the generalized emotion and lack of detailed analysis of the lover's feelings in the "songs" actually represent a step forward in Roethke's movement from confinement in the self toward love. Freer points out that the love "songs" do not include Roethke's "jumping from one state of consciousness to another, a mode that was essential to the psychological problems of the middle poems." This could be a limitation if we assume that Roethke's "consciousness jumping" is *per se* more true to his own experience than the other mode of writing. But it seems natural to conclude that the love "songs" do not work the way the earlier poems did because the poet's relation to the problems of love has changed, that the new style reflects new feelings. The fact that the love "songs" are largely traditional, generalized lyrics does not mean that they are really "love poems to poetry," as Freer suggests, but rather that the poet has achieved the confidence that allows him to view love not as a challenge but as part of the human condition and to "sing" about it as poets before him have done. If Roethke's goal in the love poems of the '50s was to "see and suffer myself / In another being, at last," the fact that the love "songs" are also "Young Girl's Songs," the first dramatic monologues about love he has written, shows clear progress in this direction. The calmer and more traditional tone of these dramatic lyrics reflects the fact that Roethke is no longer interested in proving that *he* can love as much as he is in showing the ways all of us deal with love, through the voice of the young girl.

This change in attitude is striking in Roethke's notebook work on the love "songs." The notebooks in which this work occurs are among Roethke's last. Dating from the 1960s, they show a new atmosphere of calm and a certain deliberate quality to the writing, which I will discuss in more detail in the next chapter. I suspect this change at least partially reflects Roethke's attainment of an element of security in his professional and emotional life which had been missing earlier. During the 1950s Roethke had developed his reputation with two volumes of new and selected work, winning both the Pulitzer Prize and the National Book Award; he had changed from a talented experimental poet to an established figure. If these successes helped prove to him that he could write, his marriage gradually showed him he could love. Though it would be an exaggeration to say that Roethke was free of self-doubt, the less frenetic quality of his notebooks of the '60s, along with his new ability to write of love as a part of general human experience, reflect the increased self-confidence as a poet and as a man he achieved over the previous decade.

The love poems of the '60s are composed in a manner fundamentally different from that of his earlier work. Instead of starting with lines and gradually defining his feelings through juxtapositions, Roethke clearly has a scene and general emotion in mind when he begins to write. This is true not only for the six poems identified as love "songs" but for all the "Love Poems" in *The Far Field* with the exception of the two that arise from Roethke's work of the '50s, "Light Listened" and "His Foreboding." The two free-verse poems in the group, "Her Longing" and "Her Time," have stylistic roots in the earlier *Meditations of an Old Woman* which lead to a few differences in compositional method from the others—most notably less deletion of specific images in revision—but Roethke's work on these poems is generally similar to that on the other love poems of the volume. On the whole, there is much less notebook work on the new love poems than on Roethke's poems of the '50s. Lines are not interchangeable and generally appear only in the context of the poems for which they are considered. The writing is more clearly separated into individual poems from the beginning and more focussed. The first notebook work on "Her Reticence," for example, shows Roethke with a definite idea of the poem's basic themes of reticence and surrender and the first five lines of the piece in what is practically their final form:

> If I could send him only
> A sleeve, and my hand in it,
> Disembodied, unbloody,
> For him to touch, caress,
> As he would or would not,—
> And my breasts, my vacant eyes.
> And my feet without shoes
> Which follow his thought
>
> Above my head, my piled hair,
> I would give him my breasts, my eyes,
> My feet without shoes,
>
> But not my whole body.

> (TR 43–200)

This new kind of work in the notebooks reflects Roethke's clearer initial sense of his feelings and goals in the love poems of *The Far Field*.

Like the notebook material for these poems, Roethke's work on specific drafts is considerably less extensive and experimental than that on the earlier love poems. Here are two drafts of "The Apparition," including the lines crossed out:

> ~~The Look~~
> ~~The Pillow~~

My pillow won't tell me
Where he has gone,
The wild-hearted one
Who took my heart whole,
With one tilt of his eye,
And with it, my soul.

~~Nor brushed my thin lips,~~   When I looked back at him,
~~With his lax finger tips,~~   My breath but a sigh.
But walked by, but walked by   He walked by, he walked by.

And I twist, and I turn
With my breasts, with my
                thighs,
On the harsh narrow bed.
And I wish myself dead,
~~O in his arms, reborn!~~
~~In his arms, in his arms,~~
~~Reborn!~~
Or in his arms, reborn!
                    (TR 18–17)

My pillow won't tell me
        Where he has gone,
The wild-hearted one
        I doted upon,
Who took my heart, whole,
And with it, my soul,

Who scorned my thin lips
        With the glance of his eyes,
And my breasts, their blue tips,
        And my smouldering thighs:
~~Till I wished myself dead~~
~~On my harsh narrow bed,~~

                        (TR 18–17)

The final text of the poem is as follows:

The Apparition

My pillow won't tell me
　Where he has gone,
The soft-footed one
　Who passed by, alone.

Who took my heart, whole,
　With a tilt of his eye,
And with it, my soul,
　And it like to die.

I twist, and I turn,
　My breath but a sigh.
Dare I grieve? Dare I mourn?
　He walks by. He walks by.

On the whole, the revision process is fairly straightforward here, especially when compared to Roethke's much more complex work on the love poems of *Words for the Wind*. In the two drafts we see some rearrangement of lines to set up different rhyme schemes, though nothing nearly as intricate as in the composition of a poem like "Words for the Wind"; Roethke eventually settles on a simple *abab* rhyme scheme, with only a slight irregularity in the first stanza. If formal devices function as a tool for discovering and clarifying feelings in the earlier poems, here their role is the more conventional one of setting up the "music" of the "song." In both its simple form and some of its diction—"And it like to die"; "My breath but a sigh"—there are suggestions of the Irish pub songs Roethke enjoyed hearing during his visits to the island of Inishbofin in 1960. A song, whether contemporary poem or Irish ballad, tends to be general, and removal of specific details is at the heart of Roethke's revisions of these love poems. The lips, the breasts, the thighs, the fingertips, even the bed, are all deleted as Roethke develops the final text of "The Apparition." The few specific images that remain—the "tilt of his eye," for example—are left to stand for a whole complex of feelings. The intricacies of these feelings cannot be developed in the song, but that is not the poet's goal. Expression of emotion rather than analysis is at the heart of the new love poems, and Roethke's revisions show him paring away extraneous details to draw into focus the actions and images that capture the central feelings.

The poem that closes "Love Poems" in *The Far Field* was among the last Roethke wrote. "Wish for a Young Wife" shows the change after his decade of work with the love poem:

Wish for a Young Wife

My lizard, my lively writher,
May your limbs never wither,
May the eyes in your face
Survive the green ice
Of envy's mean gaze;
May you live out your life
Without hate, without grief,
And your hair ever blaze,
In the sun, in the sun,
When I am undone,
When I am no one.

While poems like "The Dream" and "Words for the Wind" trace the poet's gradual awareness of being in love and the wonder of it, "Wish for a Young Wife" is an actual expression of love; the self is no longer in the forefront, and the poet can even look on his own death with some equanimity. This is a poem Roethke could not have written in the '50s. Its movement outward from the self is founded on the confidence he gained through the process of clarifying and developing feelings in the earlier work. In the seminar on identity he attended during the last year of his life, the poet claimed that "the self can be found in love, in human, mutual love, in work that one loves" (SP 26). Roethke's work on the love poems, from "The Vigil" through "Wish for a Young Wife," shows his movement beyond the isolated self to a deeper grounding of identity in love.

CHAPTER SEVEN

"All Journeys... Are the Same":

Meditations of an Old Woman
and *North American Sequence*

If Roethke's formal love poems of the 1950s represent one kind of movement away from "the personal myth" (SL 173), the major sequence he worked on in this decade, *Meditations of an Old Woman,* shows another response to the problem of the isolated self: the extended dramatic monologue. As in Roethke's middle period, the sequence of multi-sectioned poems in free verse is an essential poetic medium in the last phase of his career; it offers the length and flexibility needed for more extensive development of themes than single poems allow. In *Meditations of an Old Woman* and *North American Sequence,* which follows it, Roethke completes what he came to call "the long journey out of the self" ("Journey to the Interior," 1. 1). Though the two sequences differ in significant ways, the central metaphor for both is the journey. As he worked with this concept through the last stage of his career, Roethke gradually found a new way of writing and a new sense of identity in writing. In this chapter I want to examine how Roethke's "long journey out of the self" developed as he composed *Meditations of an Old Woman* and *North American Sequence.*

Before we look at the origins of this journey in *Meditations,* it is important to consider this group of dramatic monologues in the context of Roethke's other sequences. While Roethke felt he was breaking into "an entirely different style" with the love poems (SL 173), his work in *Meditations of an Old Woman* has clear stylistic and structural similarities to the earlier *Praise to the End!* sequence. In essence,

Roethke's work on *Meditations* in the mid-1950s represents a transition between the composition of *Praise to the End!* in the late '40s and *North American Sequence* in the late '50s and early '60s. Roethke himself noted one of the most obvious similarities between *Praise to the End!* and *Meditations of an Old Woman,* his "technique of developing themes alternately" (SP 58). Roethke's love poems, as we have seen, do not allow for extensive development of more than one theme; in writing them he generally discovered his central emotional tone and then unified the poem around that. As the Irish poet Seamus Heaney points out, for Roethke "love and lyric are modes of staying the confusion and fencing off emptiness"; in these poems Roethke "employs the artificer's resources of meter, stanza and rhyme to conduct himself and the poem towards a provisional statement."[1] The old woman's poems, on the other hand, are not primarily statements of feeling but rather "meditations," and their length, free verse, and multi-sectioned structure augment the fluctuating play of ideas and moods which is at the heart of the meditational process. This alternation between central themes—acceptance of old age and rage against it, personal isolation and social concerns, spiritual development and regression—creates the characteristic movement of these poems, described by various critics as "circling," "resonating" and, perhaps most accurately, "rocking."[2] This "rocking" back and forth is a slower movement than the "spring and rush of the child" (SP 41) that animates *Praise to the End!*, yet both groups share a quality of cyclic progress through alternation of themes.

Roethke's progress in completing *Meditations of an Old Woman* is itself broadly cyclic. In its first version, published in 1957 in the English edition of *Words for the Wind,* the sequence included only four poems; "Her Becoming" was added to the American edition the following year. "Her Becoming," with its scene of ecstatic illumination in a time "when reality comes closer" (3. 1), its assertion of the old woman's ability to love (3. 41–42) and her confident sense of identity—"I am benign in my own company" (4. 2)—is a more clearly affirmative poem than those written before it; Karl Malkoff calls it the "high point" of the old woman's spiritual journey.[3] Written last, "Her Becoming" incorporates the spiritual progress the old woman has made over the course of the original four-poem sequence. But, as we have seen before in Roethke's arrangement of the "Lost Son" sequence, the poet is not content to let such positive "final" visions rest. As he did earlier with "A Field of Light," Roethke places "Her Becoming" not at the end of the sequence but in the middle, where the affirmative vision is brought into juxtaposition with the loneliness and self-doubt of "Fourth Meditation" and the spiritual exhaustion of "perpetual beginnings" in "What Can I Tell My Bones?" (1. 23). Though *Meditations of an Old Woman* is shorter and considerably less complex in its compositional history than the "Lost Son" sequence or *Praise to the End!*, it develops like the earlier sequences from a cyclic process in which new work interacts with old and initial conclusions are re-examined in altered contexts.

There are also stylistic similarities among the sequences, seen most clearly in the more ecstatic passages of *Meditations*. The conclusion of "I'm Here," for example, would not seem out of place in "I Cry, Love! Love!" or the other adult poems of *Praise to the End!*:

> What's weather to me? Even carp die in this river.
> I need a pond with small eels. And a windy orchard.
> I'm no midge of that and this. The dirt glitters like salt.
> Birds are around. I've all the singing I would.
> I'm not far from a stream.
> It's not my first dying.
> I can hold this valley,
> Loose in my lap,
> In my arms.
>
>   If the wind means me,
>   I'm here!
>   Here.
>
>   (5. 1–12)

The gradual shortening of the lines as the poem approaches its end is seen in almost all the *Praise to the End!* poems— Roethke himself described it as "an effect I have become inordinately fond of" (SP 82)—and the repetition of a central word in the last two lines is a technique used previously in both "O Lull Me, Lull Me" and "Bring the Day!" The fragmentary, largely end-stopped lines, the short, disconnected sentences, the symbolically charged natural images— "eels," "birds," a "stream"— and the heavy reliance on "I" in this passage give the effect· of condensed dramatic expression, the

"psychic shorthand" (SP 42) we recognize from *Praise to the End!*
Brief passages like this one occur throughout the *Meditations,* particularly when the speaker is excited. The rapid-fire quatrains of Part
3 of "Her Becoming," the conclusion of "Fourth Meditation," and the
penultimate stanza of "What Can I Tell My Bones?" are other examples of work in the style of *Praise to the End!*

But as these passages point back to the work of the '40s, others
look ahead to the calmer, less fragmentary, more descriptive style of
North American Sequence:

> As when silt drifts and sifts down through muddy pond-water,
> Settling in small beads around weeds and sunken branches,
> And one crab, tentative, hunches himself before moving along the
>   bottom,
> Grotesque, awkward, his extended eyes looking at nothing in
>   particular,
> Only a few bubbles loosening from the ill-matched tentacles,
> The tail and smaller legs slipping and sliding slowly backward—
> So the spirit tries for another life,
> Another way and place in which to continue;
> Or a salmon, tired, moving up a shallow stream,
> Nudges into a back-eddy, a sandy inlet,
> Bumping against sticks and bottom-stones, then swinging
> Around, back into the tiny maincurrent, the rush of brownish-white
>   water,
> Still swimming forward—
> So, I suppose, the spirit journeys.
>   ("First Meditation," 3. 1–14)

The long, more enjambed lines; the extended simile in one lengthy
sentence; the attention to small, not overtly symbolic details; and the
calm, reflective speaking voice create an overall effect of slow ease
not seen in the earlier sequences. The changes in style between different passages in the *Meditations* augment these poems' "rocking"
movement and the development of alternate themes. They also reflect
the beginnings of a change in Roethke's compositional methods which
culminates in *North American Sequence.* Generally, the more dramatic passages in the *Praise to the End!* mode tend to be constructed
largely from separate lines culled from different notebooks, as

Roethke had done earlier; the passages pointing toward *North American Sequence* have their origins not primarily in individual lines but in larger descriptive units in the notebooks. We will examine this development in the writing process in more detail when we consider the composition of *North American Sequence*.

These descriptive passages reveal an obvious stylistic contrast between Roethke's sequences of the '40s and those of the following decade. An even more significant difference between *Meditations of an Old Woman* and *Praise to the End!* is Roethke's use of the dramatic monologue. Though Roethke himself warned against identifying the speaker of *Praise to the End!* too closely with the poet (SP 10), he also referred to the sequence as a "spiritual autobiography" (SP 58). As we have seen in the composition of "Where Knock Is Open Wide," a key element in the development of the speaker's consciousness is Roethke's personal memory; the references to greenhouses, dead fathers, and other specific autobiographical facts in the sequence as a whole make it clear that these poems are not dramatic monologues in the conventional sense. If Roethke's struggle to develop the speaker's voice and character in *Praise to the End!* was essentially a process of self-discovery, the creation of the old lady who speaks *Meditations* is something quite different. Roethke had felt a drive toward the dramatic monologue since the completion of *Praise to the End!* in 1951; it is a natural direction for a poet who wants to get away from "the personal myth." He refers to this dramatic impulse at the end of his "Open Letter" (SP 43), and in a letter to Kenneth Burke written just after his application for a Ford Foundation grant in 1952, he speaks of "Old Lady's Winter Words," a precursor of the *Meditations,* as fulfilling Burke's "prophecy" that Roethke would move toward more specific characters in his poems (SL 171). Burke's prediction is announced at the end of his "Vegetal Radicalism" essay and is based on a distinction between Roethke's "personification" of largely abstract qualities like sexual desire or the feminine in the images of *Praise to the End!* and the "personalization" Burke sees emerging in the newer work. In the "personalization" process characters and objects in the poem no longer serve primarily as general symbols for aspects of the poet's own psyche but rather have an existence of their own, an individual reality apart from whatever symbolic value we may find in them. Thus, as Burke notes, the student in "Elegy for Jane" has an identity apart from Roethke's own desires and feelings in a way that the female presences who appear in *Praise to the End!* do not.[4]

The creation of a character apart from his own life did not come easily to a poet who had spent the previous decade examining his past. The fact that Roethke chose a figure different from himself in age, sex, and experience and attempted to characterize her not from his own viewpoint but through the dramatic monologue shows the depth of his interest in going beyond the bounds of his own identity. His early notebook work in this area is quite stiff. One attempt at beginning "Old Lady's Winter Words" starts "Who can say / What an old lady remembers?" (TR 38–121)— obviously the poet cannot say at this point, though he clearly wants to. In several passages of the notebook work on *Meditations* he falls back into a third-person narration of events (TR 40–147, 40–155), apparently unable to capture the old lady's own voice. When Roethke fails in this way, it is most often because he is trying too hard; as the question I cited indicates, he often attempts to take on the mystery of another identity too straightforwardly in his drive to go beyond the personal. We have seen this problem before when Roethke tried to define his childhood relation to his parents in the unsuccessful "I know three names" passage. This "head-on" approach reflects the poet's lack of experience with new material and, I think, the urgency of his desire to get something on the page. When the speaker in "First Meditation" says, "I need an old crone's knowing" (1. 19), it could be Roethke himself talking. His need to approach experience from a perspective different from his own, to define an entity outside the self, leads him to certain central questions over and over, perhaps the most obvious of which is "What is it to be a woman?" from "Fourth Meditation" (2. 1). This questioning is reminiscent of Roethke's early attempts at engaging memory in "On the Road to Woodlawn," but there is an added element of difficulty here because the question, unlike the ones about the funeral, literally cannot be answered by a man; in one notebook it seems almost a cry of frustration (TR 40–159).

One technique Roethke developed for alleviating the problem of heavy-handedness in defining the old woman's character was the use of the designation "O.L." ("Old Lady") for selected passages in the notebooks. This simple notation allowed the poet to write rapidly and more or less freely as he had earlier in his work on *Praise to the End!*, without worrying whether his lines were suitable for the sequence or not. When Roethke felt his writing was approaching the old lady's voice he would note it, then move on to other work. Not all of *Meditations* was written in this way, but it is clear that Roethke relied heavily on the technique as a way to circumvent his initial self-consciousness in dealing with a voice and character not his own.

As we might expect, the different *Meditations* have common origins in the notebooks, and the "O.L." passages were gathered along with others and arranged into separate poems in the manner of Roethke's work on *Praise to the End!* There is also some selection of individual lines in a re-reading of the notebooks, but this is less extensive than in the composition of the earlier sequences. More common is the complete or partial rewriting of a central scene; different versions of the bus trip in "First Meditation," for example, appear in at least four notebooks (TR 39–125, 39–133, 40–151, 40–155). There is a kind of selection process at work here too, but new material arises within an already established context and the resulting passages in the finished texts are correspondingly less fragmentary than those put together from individually selected lines. As I have mentioned, this technique points forward to Roethke's work on *North American Sequence*. Ironically, it is the last *Meditation* to be completed, the one closest chronologically to the beginnings of *North American Sequence*, that relies most heavily on the selection of single lines from different contexts. Composed separately from the other four *Meditations*, "Her Becoming" is a kind of pastiche of "leftovers" from Roethke's earlier work; it includes material deleted from the other *Meditations* in revision as well as individual lines derived from notebook work on "Four for Sir John Davies"—"Ask all the mice who caper in the straw" (4. 1, TR 39–126)—the unpublished "Song for Middle Age"—"What lover keeps his song?" (3. 39, TR 23–62)—and other poems. Perhaps the fact that Roethke had to resort to this kind of "scavenging" to complete the piece helped convince him to limit the sequence to five poems.

Roethke's ability to work with larger units and avoid excessive reliance on selection of single lines for the first four *Meditations* he wrote is based on his early awareness of certain focal points in the sequence as a whole. These include scenes—the sea in Part 3 of "First Meditation," the windstorm at the end of Part 1 of "What Can I Tell My Bones?"—narratives like the "queen of the vale" memory in Part 2 of "I'm Here"; and speeches, such as the attack on superficial women in Part 2 of "Fourth Meditation." One of the earliest of these focal points to arise in the process of composition, and one of the most important, is the journey which eventually becomes Part 2 of "First Meditation." Roethke's first attempts with the scene, like his beginning work on capturing the old woman's character, tend to be literal and straightforward, as in this early version:

> Hamburger beacons.
> Rolling over the rock-tilts, the eight
> Tires spraying the loose shale,
> In and out of the stony passes,
> Where the snow blows
> Off the plateau's face
> Half the winter.
> Between the tumbleweed
> Stuck under stumps,
> And haphazard fences.
>
> With a sharp keeling
> Around, the bus turns
> Into the moon, live
> As a new ship, riding
> A long roll of water
> The highway pitching
> Us up and easy
> While the old lady
> Hunts for her dirty
> Peppermints, lolling
> With her string-bag
> And the little boy climbs
> Backward, his face flashing
> For a high truck's light
>
> (TR 40–155)

This passage, dated July 28, 1951, contains a good deal of accurate and fairly vivid writing, some of which will survive in the finished text. But the perspective is largely external at this point; we are given little sense of a particular character speaking this passage or the meaning of what she experiences. The short, often enjambed lines create a great sense of physical movement but allow little room for thoughts or feelings.

Roethke's understanding of the meaning of this experience comes considerably later. Re-reading a notebook in April, 1953, he marked this brief passage for special attention: "To go back to go forward— / That is the meaning of journeys" (TR 39–140). A later draft of the scene begins to incorporate the poet's new insights into the experience:

Often I think of myself as riding,
Alone, on a bus through Western country;
I sit up in front, close to the driver
When we veer and sway along on a rolling plain toward mountains,
And lull into a half-sleep, I become aware of my companions:
The child, restive, with its angular mother,
The old lady with a string bag smelling of
When all the talk subsides, the obvious chatter,
And we bounce along, rolling down into gullies,
Then up again, the lights tilting skyward,
And perhaps the drunken soldier wakes, and stares into the
            moonlight,
The old lady fumbles in her string bag for another peppermint:
Silent, nevertheless we break from our isolation;
While the gravel raps against the heavy fenders,
And the road straightens out onto a long plateau,
And the East gradually brightens;
We ride, we ride,
Into morning.

(TR 40–151)

The lines become longer, the tone more meditative as the poet begins to develop the speaker's consciousness in the scene. We also start to see the alternation between feelings of isolation and a sense of community which will become a central theme in the sequence as a whole.

But even more significant is what follows this passage in the notebook:

I remember two birds, song sparrows,
The one shuttling outside, high on top of a long greenhouse,
Its mate answered from within, on a wire strung from a pipe

Close to the air-vent;
Half the morning they sang,
While the white clouds rolled over from the West,
The elms and cedars threw up their violent shadows
And, late in the afternoon, the men carried out the earth from an
    older greenhouse,
All day the wheelbarrows creaking up and down the plank-ways;
And the heat so great even the Mexicans splashed themselves with
    water,
And a tension grew among the men, an intolerable tension,
As if it was too much to go on bearing out the dead earth,
Gray, sweated and dead, pitted and pocked like concrete,
And finally, one man ran down the road screaming and swearing

                                        (TR 40–151)

Like the passage before it, this scene approaches the final version in
Part 2 of "First Meditation" in style and narrative perspective. More
importantly, its relation to the bus ride preceding it in the notebook
develops Roethke's new sense of the dual nature of the journey, that
going "forward" in space is connected to going "back" in time through
memory. In the final version of the bus ride, the central relation
between forward and backward motion is emphasized at the beginning
and end of the stanza that links the trip and the memory:

All journeys, I think, are the same:
The movement is forward, after a few wavers,
And for a while we are all alone,
Busy, obvious with ourselves,
The drunken soldier, the old lady with her peppermints;
And we ride, we ride, taking the curves
Somewhat closer, the trucks coming
Down from behind the last ranges,
Their black shapes breaking past;
And the air claps between us,
Blasting the frosted windows,
And I seem to go backward,
Backward in time:

                                        (2. 7–19)

In the published text, Roethke concludes Part 2 of the poem with a final stanza that comments on the two preceding scenes, the bus ride and the greenhouse. "Journey within a journey" (2. 29), the stanza begins, drawing attention to the two forms of "travel" here: the external journey forward through space, which is associated with a Western landscape and social interactions; and the interior journey back through time, which is focussed largely on individual experience and is rooted in Roethke's memories of Michigan and the greenhouse.

The relation between these two journeys will become increasingly significant as Roethke goes on to write *North American Sequence*. Though this interaction in *Meditations of an Old Woman* is rudimentary, Roethke's development of it raises two important points. The first is that the external journey initiates the internal one; it is only after Roethke begins to capture the actual physical nature of the bus ride that the memory occurs. There is considerably more to this memory than the passage I have cited; following the bus ride in the notebook are several pages of personal remembrance, including a story of the poet's mother going across town to get him a "war-time chicken," a memory of riding in a truck with his father, and a detailed description of the death of a family friend. The dramatic-monologue format breaks down completely as the interior journey becomes dominant. What happens here is broadly parallel to what goes on in the composition of the sequence as a whole: In attempting to move outside himself through the dramatic monologue, Roethke continually found himself delving more deeply into his own experience.

William Carlos Williams' response to *Meditations* in a letter sheds some light on this paradoxical process:

> It's a beautiful and skillful thing, wholly satisfactory. You've got rid of your self consciousness in inventing— in invention, by adopting a dramatis persona, a "real" fiction: the old woman. You have been able to forget yourself in "her." The result is [it] liberates yourself.
>
> (TR 14–26)

The process Williams describes— escape from self-consciousness through concentration on something outside the self— is a familiar one; the poet's attention to formal effects in the love poems, his use of nonsense lines in writing *Praise to the End!*, and the extended "looking" at external objects in the composition of the greenhouse poems have all performed a similar function. But *Meditations of an Old Woman* differs from the earlier poems in that we do not see the specific fruits of this "self-liberation" directly in the published text; the memories in the notebook, as well as many of the more concrete details in the passage I have cited, could not be included in the final version without destroying the dramatic-monologue format. Despite the self-discovery involved in the writing process, Roethke retained his primary interest in the development of a speaker apart from himself.

How successful the poet was in achieving his goal is open to question. We have seen passages in *Meditations* that might have been spoken by the young man in *Praise to the End!*, and Jay Parini argues that the voice behind the sequence is more Roethke's than an old woman's.[5] John Wain, on the other hand, finds the speaker clearly feminine but her concerns those of Roethke.[6] The difficulty of determining the speaker's identity with certainty here points to the complex mixture of personal and external aspects in the poems. Despite Roethke's exclusion of more personal notebook material like the memory of riding in his father's truck or the "war-time chicken" incident, the final text of *Meditations* still contains much that belongs more to Roethke than to his old woman—the greenhouse, the familiar ecstatic harmony with nature—as well as lines like "What is it to be a woman?" or "I need an old crone's knowing," in which the poet's face is visible behind the dramatic mask. For Roethke, a "pure" dramatic monologue was impossible; the old lady's bus ride leads inevitably to the poet's own memories.

The process of the interior journey arising from external description will become increasingly important in the composition of *North American Sequence*. The second aspect of the notebook work on *Meditations* I want to discuss also presages the later sequence; it is the presence of death in the interior journey. In the memory passage I have cited, the "dead earth" the men are "bearing" away from the "older greenhouse" creates "an intolerable tension," and the description of the death of a family friend later in this notebook includes graphic references to a "thickened, purple and distended tongue" and skin blotches (TR 40–151). None of these details appear in the published text; like the more personal memories, they do not fit the dramatic-monologue format. Though death is a central concern in *Meditations*, its particular connection to the interior journey of memory could not be developed in the final version of the sequence. Working with a speaker different from himself, Roethke had to consider death as part of the old lady's experience, where it is bound up naturally with worries about the future, rather than as part of his own journey back to the past. In the published text death tends to be a challenging presence, as when "the dead make more impossible demands from their silence" in "Fourth Meditation" (1. 19) or when the old woman finds she no longer dreams of the dead in her triumph at the end of the sequence ("What Can I Tell My Bones?," 3. 11); it does not arise from memory as it does in the excluded notebook material. There is a nostalgic sense of loss associated with the past in these poems, but it is not until Roethke drops the persona of the old lady in poems like "The Far Field" and "Journey to the Interior" from *North American Sequence* that the connection between the interior journey and death becomes clear.

While Roethke's use of the dramatic monologue in *Meditations* limits his development of a key aspect of the interior journey, the poet was able to work somewhat more extensively with the complementary movement outward. As I mentioned, the external journey is associated not with memory but with physical travel and human interactions. An element of social criticism surfaces at various points in the published text: the evocation of "waste lonely places" in Part 4 of "First Meditation," the bleak vision of superficiality and "machines" in Part 2 of "Her Becoming," the attack on "ritualists of the mirror" and other of "the self-involved" in Part 2 of "Fourth Meditation." In the unpublished draft and notebook material Roethke's interest in using the old woman to comment on American society is even clearer. Interspersed among notebook work on *Meditations* are sections of what would eventually become "A Tirade Turning," Roethke's satiric essay on "my more tedious contemporaries" (SP 151; TR 40–143, 41–174), and a draft of "What Can I Tell My Bones?" has the old woman giving "the back of my tongue" to "my contemporaries" (TR 24–65). The long passage criticizing vain women in "Fourth Meditation" originally extended the attack to the American scene in general with this stanza:

> Beyond the raw ends of our provincial cities,
> Beyond the bleak sheds of our desolation,
> Beyond the miserable hutches and shacks of our wind-bitten
> > prairies,
> Beyond the sour streets, the tin cans and neon, the oily detritus,

Beyond the hideous and immaculate suburbs:

(TR 19–52)

However, this external work, like aspects of the interior journey, does not finally meet the demands of the dramatic monologue. The rhetorical parallelism, cataloguing, and supremely confident use of "our" create a broad, authoritative tone which seems too weighty for the old woman's lively sensibility. Roethke eventually deleted this stanza for being "too Whitmanesque" and for detracting from the speaker's central focus on women (TR 149–9). Though the dramatic monologue allows Roethke to develop external social criticism more freely than he can his own personal memories, the voice of the speaker still imposes limitations. *North American Sequence* has its origins in Roethke's attempt to remove these limitations and speak directly about America.

The change from working within the dramatic-monologue format in *Meditations* to developing a less limiting, more direct voice in *North American Sequence* is not clear-cut. There is a considerable overlap in Roethke's work on the more external sections of "Her Becoming," the last of the *Meditations* to be written, and "The Longing," the first poem of the new sequence. From the discarded lines I have just cited, for example, the poet ended up using "the bleak sheds of our desolation" for "Her Becoming" (2. 12) and the concept of "raw" cities for "The Longing" (1. 15). The following notebook passage shows even more clearly how the attack on superficial, mechanized life in Part 2 of "Her Becoming" is intertwined with the opening scene of "The Longing":

> Though money keeps from us the greasy edge of violence
> Fetor of cockroaches, dead fish,
> Worse than castoreum of mink or weasels;
> Agony of crucifixion on barstools.
> Saliva dripping warm from microphones,
> Machines, machines, loveless, temporal,
> Rivers rancid from grease and petrol,
> Vaults, ledgers, files, second-class mail, mirrors
> Mutilated souls in cold morgues of obligation

(TR 41–174)

Lines two through five here appear in "The Longing" (1. 3–6), while the sixth and ninth turn up in "Her Becoming" (2. 15–16). Essentially the same scene is behind the external work in both poems.

By the time "Her Becoming" is completed and placed in the middle of the *Meditations* sequence, the element of social criticism does not predominate in the poem. The attack on modern civilization at the end of Part 2 in the finished text becomes an extension of the old woman's more personal anxieties as the poem focusses on the psychic progress noted in its title. Limited by the dramatic-monologue format, "Her Becoming" and the sequence as a whole could examine the problems of an individual character but could not satisfy Roethke's growing desire to examine larger social issues. In a grant application made a few months after the publication of the final five-poem version of *Meditations of an Old Woman,* the poet listed as his first priority "A sequence of serious poems beginning with a long dirge which will express through suggestive and highly charged symbolical language the guilts we as Americans feel as a people for our mistakes and misdeeds in history and in time" (SL 224–225). This is a large order, which Roethke, of course, never filled. But his claims here go beyond mere application hyperbole to point to a new development in his progress beyond "the personal myth." In a notebook of the late '50s Roethke identified a confusion between self and speaker as a central problem for "the poet in mid-career": "All his masks begin to disappear or he begins to disappear before all his masks" (TR 41–186). Though he had tried to eliminate passages of personal memory and keep the dramatic "mask" as separate from himself as possible in *Meditations,* the concerns of these poems were still very much Roethke's own, as critics like Parini and Wain have noted. The poet's frustration at the lack of clear distinctions between his own feelings and those of his speaker comes out in a letter to Ralph Mills, in which Roethke insists that the old lady is "a dramatic character, not just me" (SL 231). "The great enemy of great art is vanity, is self-hood," Roethke wrote in a notebook of this period (TR 41–173), and it is clear that the enemy had not been completely subdued in *Meditations of an Old Woman.*

In the new work Roethke hoped to avoid the charge of vanity and resolve the confusion between speaker and self by making the concerns of the poem entirely external. The speaker and the poet would be identical—no awkward masks—but the subject matter would be too broad and historically significant to be viewed as merely personal, and the poet would be seen not primarily as an individual but as a representative of the American people. In this way Roethke could escape the limits of the dramatic monologue without falling back into "the personal myth." The epic qualities Hugh Staples notes in *North American Sequence* would, of course, augment this new concept of the poet's role;[7] the objective authority and relative anonymity of the epic narrator clearly appealed to Roethke at this point. As with Roethke's drive to create a genuine dramatic character in the *Meditations,* his success in achieving this goal is open to question, but his intentions are clear. "I'm trying to say something about America," Roethke wrote in a letter (TR 149–33).

This sense of the poet as speaker for a nation begins to emerge in the "Beyond" passage cited earlier, with its repeated use of a general American "our." The poem "Dirge," completed in the late '50s, shows further development of the long lines, rhetorical repetition, and Whitmanesque catalogues of images that go along with this new mode of writing (SL 233–234). While "Dirge" graphically illustrates the horrors of American military action in Korea, the poem lacks a sense of the historical context behind the atrocities and presents no solution to the problem other than a prayer for forgiveness. In his work on "The Longing" Roethke began to expand his sense of American guilt and work toward an image which would counter the bleakness and brutality of modern existence. Several notebooks include reading notes on books about American Indian life as well as drafts of the scene that concludes the poem (TR 41–181, 41–182, 41–184). On its most external level, "The Longing" is based on a dichotomy between the lonely mechanized world of modern America that opens the poem and the community of Indians in nature that concludes it, with the poet choosing the latter: "I'll be an Indian" (3. 20). But this simple dichotomy does not take us very far in reading the poem, and it did not take Roethke very far in writing it. As we have seen in the composition of *Meditations,* the external journey is bound up with interior movement; Roethke's desire to write about America was soon complicated by a need to write about himself.

Though the old lady's bus ride reveals the basic connection between the internal and external journeys, it is not until *North American Sequence* that Roethke develops the complexities of this interaction. Before we look at the changes in writing methods behind the later sequence, it is important to consider the relation between the two journeys in the finished text. In the final version of "The Longing," the bleak American scene which opens the poem is interrupted by the question "How to transcend this sensual emptiness?" (1. 12). As Karl Malkoff notes, this vacuity is not only a quality of the "raw cities" (1. 15) and saliva-dripping microphones (1. 5) of modern American life but also reflects an individual lethargy brought out in the last stanza of Part 1:[8]

> And the spirit fails to move forward,
> But shrinks into a half-life, less than itself,
> Falls back, a slug, a loose worm
> Ready for any crevice,
> An eyeless starer.
>
> (1. 19–23)

As the old lady put it in the first *Meditation,* "The spirit moves, but not always upward" (1. 8). The parallel between spiritual regression and a kind of devolution toward more primitive biological forms is a familiar one; the "eyeless starer" is a denizen of "The Pit" of "The Lost Son," the realm of "Mother Mildew" (2. 8) which Roethke associated with "physical and psychic exhaustion" (SP 38). In the notebook in which the opening scene of "The Longing" is developed, Roethke delves further into the exhaustion with references to "the soul at a still-stand"—a line which will eventually be used for "Journey to the Interior" (3. 3)—and "Life settling into roots, a winter-change" (TR 41–174). The movement here is interior and regressive, from the plant to the roots and then presumably back to the "dead earth." Though this "winter-change" could lead to a psychic rebirth in the kind of cyclic progress we have seen in *Praise to the End!,* Roethke's drive for an external poem at this point in his career will not allow him merely to wait for "spring." To do so would be to surrender to the "undertow" of self-contempt Carolyn Kizer mentioned (TR 8–28), instead of dominating it in the act of writing. *North American Sequence* as a whole represents the poet's struggle with "the worm's advance and retreat" ("The Long Waters," 2. 2) as he fights the psychic regression which threatens his progress outward from the self.

Contrasting to this spiritual lethargy and regression into half-life is the concept of the "journey out of the self." This idea first arises in the same notebook as the early "still-stand" passages (TR 41–174), and eventually becomes the opening line in the key transitional poem of *North American Sequence,* "Journey to the Interior":

> In the long journey out of the self,
> There are many detours, washed-out interrupted raw places
> Where the shale slides dangerously
> And the back wheels hang almost over the edge
> At the sudden veering, the moment of turning.
> Better to hug close, wary of rubble and falling stones.
> The arroyo cracking the road, the wind-bitten buttes, the canyons,
> Creeks swollen in midsummer from the flash-flood roaring into the
>   narrow valley.
> Reeds beaten flat by wind and rain,
> Grey from the long winter, burnt at the base in late summer.
> —Or the path narrowing,
> Winding upward toward the stream with its sharp stones,
> The upland of alder and birchtrees,
> Through the swamp alive with quicksand,
> The way blocked at last by a fallen fir-tree,
> The thickets darkening,
> The ravines ugly.

(I. 1–17)

There is considerable disagreement among critics about how "Journey to the Interior" works. Rosemary Sullivan's argument that "the long journey out of the self is paradoxically a journey to the interior"[9] seems to disregard Roethke's assertion that the interior journey is not the main path but rather a dangerous "detour." James McMichael sees the two journeys as antithetical, noting that, for the interior journey, "the ultimate destination of the self, regardless of its caution, is its own annihilation."[10] The detour described in Part I of "Journey to the Interior" leads to a literal dead end of "quicksand," "fallen fir-trees" and "darkening" thickets. The presence of death in the journey to the interior is even more clear in the second section of the poem, where the interior journey begins its characteristic movement back in time:

> I remember how it was to drive in gravel,
> Watching for dangerous down-hill places, where the wheels whined
>   beyond eighty—
> When you hit the deep pit at the bottom of the swale,

The trick was to throw the car sideways and charge over the hill, full
    of the throttle.
Grinding up and over the narrow road, spitting and roaring.
A chance? Perhaps. But the road was part of me, and its ditches,
And the dust lay thick on my eyelids,—Who ever wore
    goggles?—
Always a sharp turn to the left past a barn close to the roadside,
To a scurry of small dogs and a shriek of children,
The highway ribboning out in a straight thrust to the North,
To the sand dunes and fish flies, hanging, thicker than moths,
Dying brightly under the street lights sunk in coarse concrete.
The towns with their high pitted road-crowns and deep gutters,
Their wooden stores of silvery pine and weather-beaten red
    courthouses,
An old bridge below with a buckled iron railing, broken by some
    idiot plunger;
Underneath, the sluggish water running between weeds, broken
    wheels, tires, stones.
                                                        (2. 1–16)

The exhilaration at the beginning of this "straight thrust to the North"
gives way to disaster, and the "idiot plunger" could very well become
the poet himself if the race back to the past were to continue. Hugh
Staples sees most of the poem as a regressive "plunge" of this sort,[11]
but there is a literal "moment of turning" away from the interior journey here that he and other critics have missed:

And all flows past—
The cemetery with two scrubby trees in the middle of the prairie,
The dead snakes and muskrats, the turtles gasping in the rubble,
The spikey purple bushes in the winding dry creek bed—
The floating hawks, the jackrabbits, the grazing cattle—
I am not moving but they are,
And the sun comes out of a blue cloud over the Tetons,
While, farther away, the heat-lightning flashes.
I rise and fall in the slow sea of a grassy plain,
The wind veering the car slightly to the right,
Whipping the line of white laundry, bending the cottonwoods apart,
The scraggly wind-break of a dusty ranch-house.

(2. 17–28)

This change in the movement of the poem is emphasized by a stanza
break setting this passage off in the first printed version.[12] The key to
the turn is in the landscape; Roethke has pulled away from the movement back north to his Michigan past and is now headed west, as the
ranch house, the dry creek bed, and the Tetons all indicate. The connection between Western country and the external journey was first
developed in the old woman's bus ride from "First Meditation," and
"Journey to the Interior" links this landscape to the poet's new sense of
external movement as a "journey out of the self." The line "I am not
moving but they are" shows the poet shifting his attention from the self
outward to the external world, in contrast to the previous interior journey where the personal ego is clearly "in the driver's seat." At the end
of this part of the poem, the road ahead is "shimmering," the interior
"detour," as if far back, "dusty" (2. 33–34); the poet has returned to
"the long journey out of the self."

Roethke's use of changes in place to signal psychic developments
is natural in a sequence for which he considered the journey "the basic
metaphor" (TR 17–17). Emphasized by repetition, three places in particular have special importance in the sequence. Michigan represents
Roethke's past; it is the destination of the interior journey. The movement toward this place we see in the first half of "Journey to the Interior" is re-enacted at the beginning of "The Far Field." The American
West is a transitional region the poet crosses on his journeys. It
appears in "The Longing" and "The Rose," as well as "Journey to the
Interior." The last section of "Journey to the Interior" is set in a landscape of "waves" (3. 6, 16) and dripping leaves (3. 11) which is the
conclusion of the external journey west, away from the Michigan past,
in the poem and the third significant place in the sequence as a whole:
the Pacific Northwest. Roethke's home since the late '40s, this region
is naturally associated with life in the present rather than memory in
the sequence. In the last stanza of "Journey to the Interior" Roethke
summarizes the progress brought about by the interaction between the
interior and external journeys:

As a blind man, lifting a curtain, knows it is morning,
I know this change:
On one side of silence there is no smile;

But when I breathe with the birds,
The spirit of wrath becomes the spirit of blessing,
And the dead begin from their dark to sing in my sleep.

(3. 23–28)

Again we see the familiar motif of the dead helping the living, the transformation of the "spirit of wrath" associated with the judging father and the poet's self-contempt into the "spirit of blessing" with its promise of nurturing and growth. In "Journey to the Interior" this transformation suggests a new sense of ease and the hope of further development as the "morning" turns into day and the "beginning" song continues. Though the journey to the interior is regressive and dangerous, the poet's confrontation with it, "The stand at the stretch in the face of death" (3. 15), eventually aids in his progress on the external journey. As Staples notes, the detour is "wrong but necessary," and the poem as a whole not only describes the detour but also traces an important "journey *from* the interior" [Staples' emphasis].[13]

Roethke's development of the journey out of the self is reflected in certain new methods of composition. A few of these first appeared in Roethke's work on *Meditations of an Old Woman,* as I have mentioned, but it is not until the composition of *North American Sequence* that the new way of writing becomes clear. The fundamental change occurs in the notebooks. Though it would be wrong to characterize any of Roethke's notebook work as orderly or systematic, the notebooks for *North American Sequence* contain more clearly deliberate work than do the earlier ones. For example, the first element of the opening of "Journey to the Interior" to arise— and one of the first elements in Roethke's work on the sequence as a whole—is not an intriguing line or a detail of description, as we might expect from Roethke's previous methods, but the central concept behind the section: "the long journey out of the self" (TR 41–174). This phrase does not come from a group of lines or a scene but rather stands on its own as a basic generalization which Roethke immediately begins to define with additional lines:

In the long journey out of the self
On the way from knowledge to love.
In the war between flesh and spirit.

(TR 41–174)

In this long journey out of the self
In the slow turning from knowledge to love—
In this wild chance of light, anarchy of sky and cloud,
The lifting, the relinquishing,
The fish-raven flying on horizontal wings
The cormorant
The rain descending on the battered statues.

                                        (TR 41–176)

Though we find passages of abstract writing like the first one here in Roethke's notebooks for *Praise to the End!*, they are generally obscure and disconnected and are used primarily for the accretion of new material, as we saw in Roethke's work with the "circularity" line from "I Cry, Love! Love!" Roethke's development of the "journey out of the self" in the first passage here is, in contrast, a straightforward attempt at defining an idea; the defining lines themselves, none of which survives in the final text, are important not so much for the material they might add to the poem as for the way they clarify and expand the concept behind the work. In these lines we see the poet defining a major goal for the whole sequence: to proceed from "knowledge," something gained by the self, to "love," a movement beyond the limitations of self. If the interior journey leads at best toward knowledge of self and past, the "journey out of the self" incorporates this knowledge and goes beyond it to reach out to the world.

The second of the two notebook passages shows the next step after a concept is defined: a gathering of physical images. Though this particular passage is fragmentary and not finally successful, we can see the beginnings of a scene here, an extended description which might have fleshed out the concept of the journey with images of birds in flight. Roethke's attempt to build a descriptive scene immediately following the conceptual lines is actually somewhat unusual in his notebook work of this period; much more common are lengthy descriptions composed separately from the conceptual framework they will eventually fill out. The Indian scene that concludes "The Longing," for example, arises after some prose notes on Indian life and is written independently of the more abstract lines defining the poet's desires which precede it in the final text (TR 41–184); and several of the physical details in the dangerous detour at the start of

"Journey to the Interior" come from a passage written separately from the lines defining it as a "journey out of the self" (TR 42–187).

The length and frequency of these descriptive passages in the notebooks for *North American Sequence* point to an ease with "pure" description not generally seen in Roethke's earlier work. The longer passages in the *Praise to the End!* notebooks tend to be either obscure, disconnected, or highly charged emotionally, with little attempt to render the details of the outside world accurately; the focus is not on the descriptive power of images but on their psychic associations, what they reveal about the self. But as Roethke begins to move beyond the limitations of self in *Meditations of an Old Woman* and *North American Sequence*, his notebooks include more and more description of things and events for their own sakes. The "master of suggestion" is going back here to the powers as a "master of description" he had developed earlier in the greenhouse poems, with the important difference that the poet is no longer depicting personal memories but rather aspects of the outside world. In one notebook from the early '60s this attention to pure description leads Roethke to a straightforward listing of nouns and adjectives related to the ocean floor under the heading "Quality of the Bottom" (TR 42–191). This quasi-scientific approach would have been impossible earlier; the poet's drive for self-discovery would have quickly turned it into Freudian word association. But by the late '50s Roethke had gone far enough beyond "the personal myth" to approach description and the world this way.

Roethke's ability to develop concepts, apart from scenes or narratives, at the beginning of composition marks another change in the fundamentals of the writing process. In the notebooks of the 1940s Roethke worked inductively, discovering the meaning of his experience as he gathered the specific details that went into it. Indeed it is hard to imagine the process of self-discovery through writing proceeding any other way. The love poems of *Words for the Wind*, with their interchangeable lines allowing for the gradual discovery and clarification of emotions, are also written largely inductively. Roethke's approach in the composition of *North American Sequence*, however, is essentially deductive. It is the concepts which organize the poems and determine which descriptive and narrative passages are appropriate, not vice-versa. Roethke can work from the general to the specific because his goal has changed from self-discovery to expression, from learning about himself and his feelings to saying what he thinks.

To say what one thinks, of course, one must think before one says; the fact that Roethke's notebook work on *North American Sequence* is less extensive, less irrational, and more deliberate than his earlier work suggests more thought *before* the writing process and less discovery *during* it. Despite the obvious stylistic differences, the notebooks for *North American Sequence* are similar to those for the poet's last love poems in this regard, reflecting Roethke's concern with expression and movement beyond the self in both cases. There is a kind of security, a general confidence that the poet can speak about large topics like love or America, behind his work on both these love poems and *North American Sequence*. The old fear of "sophomoric straining" (TR 20–5) has been overcome.

Because of Roethke's largely deductive method in the composition of *North American Sequence,* the "wait" between the generation of material in the notebooks and its selection during re-reading is considerably less important than it had been earlier, and on the whole the distinction between the first and second stages of composition is blurred. Some of the notebooks contain the kind of work with large units of draft material Roethke had previously done only after lines had been selected and transferred to separate sheets (TR 41–185, 42–187). The early development of concepts and the ease of writing scenes and narratives facilitates this change. The final text is developed by accumulation and arrangement of these draft units. At this third stage of composition, Roethke's work on *North American Sequence* is broadly similar to that on earlier sequences, although like the work in the notebooks it is less extensive and less experimental than his work on *Praise to the End!* With important concepts and central lines determined early in the writing process, Roethke polishes and arranges the larger units, in some cases removing whole scenes and replacing them with others that work within the conceptual framework more effectively. The idea of Roethke as a boy "learning of the eternal" (2. 6) in Part 2 of "The Far Field," for example, is brought out through a memory of seeing dead animals near the greenhouse; in an alternate version the death of the poet's great-grandmother is described (TR 19–38). Both passages develop essentially the same point, but the one about the great-grandmother does not have the references to nature or the meditative tone that would fit the rest of this section of the poem and is thus discarded.

The third stage of composition for *North American Sequence* involves not only selection and arrangement of scenes but also some small but significant work with linebreaks and stanzas. Here are two fragments from Roethke's work on the opening of "Meditation at Oyster River," each followed by the published version of the passage:

Over the low, elephant-colored rocks
Come the first tide-ripples, moving,
Almost without sound, toward me,
Running along the narrow furrows of the shore,
The rows of dead clam shells,
Then a runnel behind me, creeping closer,
Alive with tiny striped fish,

(TR 21–38)

Over the low, barnacled, elephant-colored rocks,
Come the first tide-ripples, moving, almost without sound,
    toward me,
Running along the narrow furrows of the shore, the rows of dead
    clam shells;
Then a runnel behind me, creeping closer,
Alive with tiny striped fish, and young crabs climbing in and out of
    the water.

(1. 1–5)

The wind slackens,
Light as a moth fanning a stone.
A twilight wind,
Light as a child's breath,
Turning not a leaf, not

(TR 21–38)

The wind slackens, light as a moth fanning a stone:
A twilight wind, light as a child's breath
Turning not a leaf, not a ripple.

(1. 17–19)

Seven lines become five and five become three as the poet makes combinations and adds details to build up the long line, dense with imagery, that is a central feature of his style in the sequence. While short lines fit the leaps of association in Roethke's earlier work, the longer line is more suited to physical description with its subtle, speech-oriented rhythms and its accumulation of concrete details. This kind of revision in linebreaks is rare in Roethke's earlier work, but in *North American Sequence* it was required to develop a unity of feeling. The calm, meditative tone such lines project is in sharp contrast to the "spring and rush" (SP 41) of the short lines of *Praise to the End!*, reflecting the difference between the nervous forays into the past and the unconscious in the earlier sequence and the slow, deliberate "journey out of the self" that is behind the later group.

Not only lines expand and grow calmer in revision; stanzas are affected too. One complete draft of "Meditation at Oyster River," which is otherwise quite close to the final text, contains four breaks between stanzas in the first, third, and fourth sections that are eventually eliminated (TR 21–38); a complete draft of "Journey to the Interior" (TR 20–55) also shows four stanza breaks not seen in the published text, and a draft of "The Longing" (TR 21–24) has three. Though this consolidating movement sacrifices some distinctions made by the breaks between stanzas, it generally serves to unify the poems by drawing attention away from changes within the numbered sections to the sections as units in themselves, many of which, in the published text, contain only one or two stanzas. In this way the movement within a given section of a poem becomes more of a piece, more a long journey than a texture of argument and counter-argument.

The final version of *North American Sequence* does not abandon the alternating development of themes or the cyclic progress we have seen in the earlier sequences, but the "swings" in this rocking movement are broader and calmer. The fragmentary passages of ecstasy and despair that characterize *Praise to the End!* and parts of *Meditations of an Old Woman* have largely vanished along with the technique of individual line selection that was at their core. In place of these passages are longer scenes, generally composed as units and integrated into the overall meaning of the poem without being reduced to "psychic shorthand." As Mills notes, "there is in every poem a substantial portion of magnificent descriptive writing, important in its links with the inner life but delightful and evocative in itself."[14] "I embrace the world," the poet claims at the end of "The Long Waters" (5. 19), and the descriptive passages show how this claim is not mere egotism. The world in *North American Sequence* exists in its own right, and the alternating movement in the sequence is not primarily between levels of individual consciousness as in *Praise to the End!* or different moods as in *Meditations,* but between the self and the world, the inner and outer journeys.

In striving to move outward toward the world, Roethke developed a new vision of self in the sequence. It is not the disembodied, bardic voice we might expect in poems about a whole continent, but rather a personal yet unself-conscious presence seen nowhere else in Roethke's work. This new voice comes out most clearly in the small phrases like "I think of," "I remember," and "I see" which often introduce the longer narrative and descriptive passages. Common as these phrases are, they show a calm, secure attitude toward the self as observer which is generally lacking in Roethke's earlier work, in which a frenetic assertion of identity along the lines of "I insist! / I am" from "Sensibility! O La!" (3. 24–25) is the prototype. Corresponding to this change is a new ability to approach the past directly, again seen most clearly in introductory phrases: "I remember how it was to drive in gravel" ("Journey to the Interior," 2.1); "And I think of roses, roses" ("The Rose," 2. 21). The link between the speaker in the present and his past is made naturally and unobtrusively. Roethke's earlier techniques for approaching the past—the two-level description of the greenhouse poems, the dramatic "tensed-up *Prelude*" of *Praise to the End!*—seem artificial and involuted in comparison. Paradoxically, it is the poet's distance from past experience in *North American Sequence* that allows for the easy commerce between past and present, self and world here. As Harry Williams notes, the repeated phrase "I think" establishes the poet's "primary mode of existence" in *North American Sequence.*[15] No longer dramatically reliving his memories and functioning simultaneously as main character and speaker as he had in *Praise to the End!*, the poet as "thinker" is set apart from his past by the concepts he has developed. These concepts, however, provide a framework of meaning which allows memories to be approached in the same direct way that descriptive scenes are approached, as illustrations and extensions of the poet's ideas. The "tensed-up *Prelude*" with "no comment; everything in the mind of the kid" (SL 148), has been replaced with poetry closer to the Wordsworthian original, in which "comments" give access to the past.

On one level, this meditative approach to past experience might appear to be a defensive maneuver, reminiscent of Roethke's emphasis on control by the conscious will in the early work: It is safe to examine one's self-destructive tendencies as long as they are clearly announced as a "detour"; the pain of youthful suffering is anesthetized when it is seen as a lesson in the "eternal." But the framework of ideas Roethke uses to deal with his past in *North American Sequence* is quite different from the tough, defensive stance he assumed in *Open House*. It is based not on a pose but on a true understanding of past experience, which would not have been possible earlier; Roethke had to relive his past in the work of the '40s before he could make sense of it in *North American Sequence*. And the way Roethke makes sense of experience in this sequence does not distort or downplay feelings for the sake of rational control. In fact, Roethke's desire to go beyond "the personal myth" and fit scenes from his past into a structure of ideas includes one particular emotional element seen rarely in his earlier work. As *North American Sequence* progresses, this element comes more and more to the surface, reaching its clearest expression in the greenhouse memory from Part 2 of "The Rose," in which the poet concludes, "What need for heaven, then, / With that man, and those roses?" (2. 26–27). As Rosemary Sullivan points out, this scene represents one of the few times in Roethke's poetry when love for the father is expressed directly, without being colored by the poet's anxieties.[16]

This direct expression of love is seen again at the conclusion of "Otto," a poem composed at the same time and in many of the same notebooks as *North American Sequence*:

> I'd stand upon my bed, a sleepless child
> Watching the waking of my father's world.—
> O world so far away! O my lost world!

In "A Greenhouse Eden," Louis Martz describes how Roethke "overcomes his embarrassment at open exclamation" in writing "Otto," noting that "the cry [at the end of the poem] is the full recognition of his true center."[17] The two-sided image of the father in the "tensed-up *Prelude*" and other poems of the 1940s is, as we have seen, a reflection of the son's psychic conflicts. By *The Far Field*, the distance Roethke has gained on his experience allows him to see the father apart from his own hopes and fears; he becomes less a symbol, more a specific mortal with, as "Otto" shows, a personal history and a name. As the father changes into what Burke would call a "personalized" individual character instead of a "personification" of the poet's anxieties, his power over the son diminishes and a genuine sense of love and loss becomes possible. The decrease in the father's power corresponds to the poet's increased self-confidence. As Roethke put it in a letter, "One lesson of maturity: there is no papa" (TR 16–42). With Papa "personalized" into Otto, the poet has changed from a troubled "lost son" to a more secure figure who can show mature feelings of love and sorrow about his dead father.

Roethke's ability to approach the past directly and express a genuine sense of loss reflects a new ease about identity which is related to his new ease in composition. Paradoxically, this acceptance of self has its origins in the poet's desire to go beyond "the personal myth." In the last poem of *North American Sequence* Roethke examines this paradox. "The Rose" was written after Roethke had thought the sequence complete; in a letter from late 1961 he refers to an American sequence with only "five longish poems" (TR 17–17), and in a later proposal for a selection of poems "The Rose" is pencilled in apart from the sequence (TR 27–14). The separation between "The Rose" and the other poems provided an element of time and personal distance which allowed Roethke to develop a new awareness of what the sequence was doing. When "The Rose" is finally incorporated in the sequence, it is placed, significantly, at the end. The kind of cycle-making we have seen previously in *Meditations of an Old Woman* and *Praise to the End!* is no longer appropriate. At this point the poet is not interested in discovering new truths through the juxtaposition of different poems but rather in stating what he has learned directly. "The Rose" is not an equal element to be brought into interaction with the other poems but a summary and extension of the sequence as a whole, a kind of coda.

Though this coda is generally similar to the other poems in *North American Sequence*—it does not appear out of place or "tacked on"— the way "The Rose" progresses shows Roethke's new understanding of the central paradox in the sequence. As we have seen, the earlier poems tend to "rock" broadly back and forth between the external journey and interior travel, between America and past experience. "The Rose" moves toward a resolution of this alternating motion through a merging of apparent opposites. The impulse toward consolidation in Roethke's work with lines and stanza breaks is extended here to include the central dichotomies on which *North American Sequence* is based. This merging process begins in the poem's opening lines:

There are those to whom place is unimportant,
But this place, where sea and fresh water meet,
Is important—

(1. 1–3)

"This place... Is important," Roethke announces, and what makes the
place important is that it is "where sea and fresh water meet." "The
Rose" is set at the end of the journey west, the "long journey out of
the self," but in its first image we are reminded of the other realm; the
fresh water comes from the interior. The westward movement of the
freshwater stream parallels Roethke's own, both in the sequence and
in his life. The opening image suggests an important aspect of the
place of "meeting" between the two realms: the interaction between
the interior and exterior worlds, the personal past and the world outside the self, is continuous and interdependent, with the stream from
the interior constantly feeding the external sea.

After the scene is established, the poet "sways outside" himself
(1. 22) and participates in a kind of nautical parallel to the old lady's
bus ride (2. 1–8) in which the self has been subsumed in "our motion"
(2. 8). This external journey stops abruptly with the appearance of the
poem's central image:

But this rose, this rose in the sea-wind,
Stays,
Stays in its true place,
Flowering out of the dark,
Widening at high noon, face upward,
A single wild rose, struggling out of the white embrace of the
          morning-glory,
Out of the briary hedge, the tangle of matted underbrush,
Beyond the clover, the ragged hay,
Beyond the sea pine, the oak, the wind-tipped madrona,
Moving with the waves, the undulating driftwood,
Where the slow creek winds down to the black sand of the shore
With its thick grassy scum and crabs scuttling back into their
          glistening craters.

(2. 9–20)

The repetition at the opening of this passage makes the main concept clear: The stasis, the rootedness of the rose is juxtaposed with the movement of the journey west, suggested here by the "sea-wind" and the waves. However, the rose is not merely an image of the past interior world set in simple contrast to the "journey out of the self." Though roses are part of the greenhouse world and depend on fresh water for life, this "single wild rose" finds its "true place" by the sea. As La Belle notes, the image links "past and present, Midwest and Northwest."[18] The significance of the rose is that it lives at the place of "meeting" between the two worlds.

When the relation of the rose to the past is developed at the end of Part 2, the whole concept of the interior journey is altered:

> And I think of roses, roses,
> White and red, in the wide six-hundred-foot greenhouses,
> And my father standing astride the cement benches,
> Lifting me high over the four-foot stems, the Mrs. Russells, and his
>   own elaborate hybrids,
> And how those flowerheads seemed to flow toward me, to beckon
>   me, only a child, out of myself.
>
> What need for heaven, then,
> With that man, and those roses?
>   (2. 21–27)

Going back into the self, the poet in memory is beckoned by the roses "out of myself." This brief foray into the past has the opposite effect from that of the interior movement seen earlier in "Journey to the Interior" and "The Far Field." It leads not to isolation and death but back out of the self to a true expression of love. With guilt and self-contempt largely overcome, the past, like the father who dwells in it, is no longer threatening. Finding his "true place" in the last poem of the sequence, Roethke has come to see that the interior world, like the freshwater stream, feeds into the outer realm, leading him to a deeper sense of self and world instead of smothering him in regression. A clear "moment of turning" is no longer necessary because the world of the past leads naturally back out to external reality.

The next section of the poem presents another version of the interior journey as the poet pursues American "sound and silence" (3. 1) eastward from the Tombstone (3. 3), through the Dakotas (3. 11) to Michigan (3. 12), moving in time from a summer of "gardens" and "raggedy lilacs" (3. 7) to winter (3. 11–12). This interior journey does not end in the silence of a stalled car in a snowdrift like Part 1 of "The Far Field" but rather in a "return to the twittering of swallows above water" (3. 16) which leads to yet another "open exclamation" of feeling: "Beautiful my desire, and the place of my desire" (3. 21). The wintry world of the past leads into spring; the desire to follow the journey back and the interior world itself are now both "beautiful." This new sense of the past and memory reflects the poet's cyclic progress through the different versions of the inner journey in the course of writing the first five poems. By the time Roethke comes to "The Rose," the journey to the interior is no longer regressive but rejuvenating; it complements and enriches the movement outward to the world which is at the heart of the sequence.

In the last section of "The Rose," Roethke focusses directly on the issue of personal identity:

> Near this rose, in this grove of sun-parched, wind-warped
>   madronas,
> Among the half-dead trees, I came upon the true ease of myself,
> As if another man appeared out of the depths of my being,
> And I stood outside myself,
> Beyond becoming and perishing,
> A something wholly other,
> As if I swayed out on the wildest wave alive,
> And yet was still.
> And I rejoiced in being what I was:
> In the lilac change, the white reptilian calm,
> In the bird beyond the bough, the single one
> With all the air to greet him as he flies,
> The dolphin rising from the darkening waves;
>
> And in this rose, this rose in the sea-wind,
> Rooted in stone, keeping the whole of light,
> Gathering to itself sound and silence—
> Mine and the sea-wind's.
>
>   (4. 10–26)

In the earlier sections of the poem Roethke showed how the interior world of the past and the self augments the outward journey; in Part 4 we find the reverse is also true: To "stand outside" oneself is to discover "the true ease" of oneself. The poet's comments in the symposium on identity shed some light on this merging of the interior and external journeys:

> It is paradoxical that a very sharp sense of the being, the iden-
> tity of some other being—and in some instances, even an inanimate
> thing—brings a corresponding heightening and awareness of one's
> own self, *and,* even more mysteriously, in some instances, a feeling
> of the oneness of the universe. (SP 25, Roethke's emphasis)

We have seen concentration on the outer world leading to heightened self-awareness in some of Roethke's earlier work; later in his comments here he refers to the Rilkean "looking" which was essential to the composition of the greenhouse poems (SP 25). But the next step, "a feeling of the oneness of the universe," is the key to the merging of inner and outer realms at the end of *North American Sequence.* If the "long journey out of the self" proceeds from "knowledge" to "love," as Roethke put it in his notebooks (TR 41–174, 41–176), the "true ease of myself" is not merely heightened self-knowledge but something more. It is characterized by "a loss of the 'I,' the purely human ego, to another center, a sense of the absurdity of death, a return to a state of innocency," according to the poet (SP 26). In going beyond the "purely human ego" and its anxieties about "becoming and perishing," the poet reaches "another center" where he can "rejoice in being" what he is; the rose at the end of the poem is alive, individual, and rooted in Roethke's own past. This new "center" is grounded in love of the external world— the landscape and creatures of the poet's America—and acceptance of self as part of that world, "a something wholly other," quite different from the ego-bound identity before the journey begins.[19] At the end of the journey, world and self, motion and stasis, present and past all merge.

Roethke did not intend this kind of all-encompassing conclusion when he began the sequence as a critical look at America; after its completion, he noted that the poems had "all turned out to be affirmative" and stressed a desire to go back to his original idea and "explore the other side of the coin" (TR 17–29). But, as Seamus Heaney points out, Roethke's basic urge was to praise, and it is through praise of external things that he achieved personal tranquility in the sequence.[20] Roethke noted the other central element of his work of the '50s and '60s when he characterized himself not only as a "poet of praise" but also a "poet of love" (SP 60). His movement away from self-discovery as a primary goal is the impetus for both the love poems and the sequences of his last period. Taken together, the two kinds of poem show the development of love in both a specific and a general sense: Roethke's union with "another being" in the love poems is expanded to include a sense of "the oneness of the universe" in *North American Sequence*.

As we have seen, this affirmative vision grows from the new modes of composition the poet developed over the last decade of his career. Freed from the tensions of continual plunges into the unconscious and the need to work in associative "psychic shorthand" to discover aspects of his identity, Roethke gradually came to write in a more relaxed, deliberate way. He began to work deductively, fitting details from his past and the world at large into a structure of ideas developed early in the writing process. Through his composition of *Meditations of an Old Woman* and *North American Sequence* Roethke attained a new perspective on his experience. His "long journey out of the self" in these sequences led him finally to a vision of self-acceptance and harmony with the world.

CHAPTER EIGHT

Conclusion

Despite Theodore Roethke's sudden death from a heart attack at
the age of fifty-five, the overall shape of his career does not have a jag-
ged edge to it. In the last three years of his life, Roethke reached the
culmination of his work in the two major modes of his last period: the
multi-sectioned, free-verse sequence and the formal lyric. We have
seen how *North American Sequence*, and "The Rose" in particular,
complete the "long journey out of the self" begun earlier in *Meditations of an Old Woman*. In a similar way "Sequence, Sometimes
Metaphysical" caps Roethke's earlier work in the love poems of
Words for the Wind. From the "dark time" of spiritual doubts that
opens "Sequence, Sometimes Metaphysical" the poet gradually
moves, as Roethke put it in a letter, "into a more human realm, into
what finally is a condition of joy" (TR 17–17). Thus the darker side of
the love poems of the '50s, which was the original impulse for the later
metaphysical work, is eventually transmuted into the affirmative
vision of the last poem of the sequence and *The Far Field* as a whole,
"Once More, the Round":

> What's greater, Pebble or Pond?
> What can be known? The Unknown.
> My true self runs toward a Hill
> More! O More! visible.
>
> Now I adore my life
> With the Bird, the abiding Leaf,
> With the Fish, the questing Snail,
> And the Eye altering all;
> And I dance with William Blake

For love, for Love's sake;

And everything comes to One,
As we dance on, dance on, dance on.

The vision of self-acceptance and oneness with the universe here echoes that at the end of "The Rose." In essence both modes of writing
pointed to the same happy conclusion. The fact that Roethke considered *Dance On, Dance On, Dance On* as a title for his last volume
from early 1962 through mid-March, 1963 shows how central this
affirmative vision was for him.[1]

What direction might Roethke's work have taken now that the
"long journey out of the self" was complete? Citing the reference to
Blake in "Once More, the Round," Jenijoy La Belle and Roy Harvey
Pearce surmise that Blakean prophetic books might have been the next
step for Roethke.[2] Though there is no work of this sort in the notebooks, the kind of poetry these two critics note would be a plausible
outgrowth of the poet's external focus and meditative style in his last
sequence. Roethke himself mentioned several goals in the last months
of his life, including poems on American history and different kinds of
dramatic work (TR 17–29, 17–30). There is little direct evidence of
work on these projects in the poet's last notebooks, but we do see
Roethke's continuing development of the traditional lyric in the mode
of the love "songs" of *The Far Field*. As I have mentioned, the poet's
ease of composition in this kind of work is a striking characteristic of
the later notebooks. This new ease, and Roethke's renewed interest in
the dramatic and the external, reflect the poet's confidence at the end
of his life. The struggle for self-acceptance was behind him, and he
was free to look outward and work more as a craftsman within a tradition than as a man driven to write by his own insecurities. And
Roethke was a happy man. In his biography Seager describes the last
two years of Roethke's life as hectic on the outside but "all calm
within,"[3] and Richard Hugo feels that Roethke's announcement of his
happiness late in life, like T. S. Eliot's, was essentially "honest."[4]

Hugo's comparison of Roethke and Eliot may seem strange, considering how vociferously Roethke attacked "Tiresome Tom" in his
letters (SL 154), but, as La Belle demonstrates, Eliot's ideas were central to Roethke's work.[5] Eliot's concept of writing as an "escape from
personality" is of particular interest:

Poetry is not a turning loose of emotion, but an escape from emotion; it is not the expression of personality, but an escape from personality. But, of course, only those who have personality and emotions know what it means to want to escape from these things.[6]

The last sentence here has special ramifications for Roethke's early work. The "long journey out of the self" is a version of Eliot's "escape from personality," but the poet first had to forge a sense of identity before he could go beyond it. In *Open House* Roethke took on the task directly, using formal techniques and a careful process of exclusion to create an identity for himself. The artificial sense of self proved inadequate, and in the 1940s Roethke developed new techniques for genuine self-discovery, including extensive Rilkean "looking" at objects and memories, cyclic patterns of writing to re-evaluate past experience and emotions, and different ways of liberating unconscious material in his notebooks. In his attempt to discover his own identity and its meaning in the middle stage of his career, Roethke was involved with exactly what Eliot says poetry is *not:* a "turning loose of emotion" and the "expression of personality." But once a sense of self was established through these means, Roethke felt the desire to escape from the merely personal Eliot notes. His progress from the early '50s on is outward from the self toward love. In writing the formal love poems Roethke moved toward emotional vulnerability and union with another person; in the two major sequences of this period the "long journey out of the self" leads eventually to a complementary sense of oneness with the universe. Compositional techniques like the interchangeable lines of the love poems and the separation between concepts and description in the sequences help keep the ego at bay to some extent, allowing the poems to develop more than just the "expression of personality." As Eliot put it, "What happens is a continual surrender of himself as he is at the moment to something which is more valuable."[7]

For Eliot, that something was the poem within the literary tradition, but for Roethke the "surrender" of self yielded not only the poem but also a new, broader sense of identity. To quote Eliot in a different context,

We shall not cease from exploration

And the end of all our exploring
Will be to arrive where we started
And know the place for the first time.

("Little Gidding," V. 26–29)[8]

Roethke's wish to be Indian rather than explorer notwithstanding, the journey beyond the self in his last period was an exploration, and its final result included a deeper, truer sense of his own origins. Paradoxically, this new sense of identity would not have been possible if Roethke had not attempted to move beyond "the personal myth" or had not been able to "surrender himself" in the process of writing. This is where the characterization of Roethke as a confessional poet shows its limitations. Indeed, the two critics who argue that Roethke is confessional both conclude that he is not finally successful.[9] Roethke's primary subject was the self, but his goal—even in his middle period— was not emotional catharsis through an exposure of his own weaknesses but deeper self-understanding and eventual self-transcendence. Robert Phillips' argument that the "concealed hordes of half-confessions" in *Praise to the End!* eventually give way to more "open and frank discussions" in "late poems" like "Meditation in Hydrotherapy" and "Lines upon Leaving a Sanitarium" assumes that Roethke wanted to be more explicit, more fully confessional, in *Praise to the End!* but could not, ignoring the fact that these two more "open and frank" poems were actually written more than ten years before *Praise to the End!* and were never chosen by Roethke for inclusion in any volume.[10] The "psychic shorthand" he used in *Praise to the End!* was designed not so much to capture specific experiences—it is much too oblique and associative for that—as the emotional and psychological forces behind them. Memory, plunges into the unconscious, and dramatic recreation of childhood experience all had their places, as we have seen, but Roethke's journey over the course of his career was not always inward, and it is the outward movement, not the presentation of purely personal material, which leads to the poet's final "condition of joy." Writing did indeed help Roethke, as he put it, "transmute and purify my 'life,' the sense of being defiled by it" (SP 15), but this transmutation did not come through a process of confession.

Hugo's idea that "a lifetime of writing was a slow, accumulative way of accepting one's life as valid"[11] fits Roethke's career more accurately than does the confessional model. In her letter to Roethke on writing and the self, Carolyn Kizer compares guilt and self-contempt to "a pair of terribly destructive wild horses who will kick their stalls to pieces and die of self-inflicted wounds unless they are led out gently and broken to harness. So you make them plough for you" (TR 8–28). Writing "transmutes" the poet's sense of inadequacy, not by exposing it, letting the self-destructive horses out of harness, but rather by *altering* it, as what Eliot called "*significant* emotion, emotion which has its life in the poem and not in the history of the poet" [Eliot's emphasis][12] gradually develops out of the poet's original feelings. In his comments on Roethke and Eliot, Hugo stresses the interaction between the mask of identity projected in a poem and the poet's own sense of self:

> The self as given is inadequate and will not do.... Every poem a poet writes is a slight advance of self and a slight modification of the mask, the one you want to be. Poem after poem the self grows more worthy of the mask, the mask comes closer to fitting the face. After enough poems, you are nearly the one you want to be, and the one you want to be closely resembles you. The happiness Eliot and Roethke spoke of is one that cannot be observed by others because it is only a different way one has come to feel about oneself.[13]

In this slow process Roethke was, as one of his "masks" put it, a "perpetual beginner" ("What Can I Tell My Bones?," 1. 2). After laboring to perfect a mask in *Open House*, he found himself going back to discover the face behind the mask in the 1940s, then back outward again to discover more complex relations between the inner and outer realms, face and mask. In each stage of his career, he developed new styles and ways of writing to deal with these "beginnings," resulting in a variety of work rare among modern poets, from traditional love lyrics to wildly experimental dramatic sequences, from intricate concrete descriptions to spare studies of philosophical concepts.

Though Roethke's different styles, particularly in his earlier work, show some elements of current literary vogues—the taut metaphysical poem of the '30s, the musical surrealism of Dylan Thomas in the next decade— Roethke's "perpetual beginnings" were not mere responses to fashion. Each new style was based on significant changes in the compositional process: a new way of writing for a new approach to experience. The different conclusions the "perpetual beginner" reached in his career reflect these changes in writing methods. When

Roethke switched, say, from striving toward a formal stanza early in the writing process to long periods of "looking," or from extended plunges into the unconscious to the generation of interchangeable iambic lines, he was not seeking a style to express ideas he already had but rather working toward a new way of thinking through writing. In his essay "A Way of Writing," the poet William Stafford clarifies the relation between process and conclusion involved here:

> A writer is not so much someone who has something to say as he is someone who has found a process that will bring about new things he would not have thought of if he had not started to say them. That is, he does not draw on a reservoir; instead, he engages in an activity that brings to him a whole succession of unforeseen stories, poems, essays, plays, laws, philosophies, religions, or—...[14]

As Roethke put it in "The Waking," "I learn by going where I have to go."

Stafford's description of this "learning by going" applies to the work of many writers, and some of the principles behind Roethke's compositional methods at different stages of his career have been shared by other poets. The commitment to the unconscious at the beginning of the writing process, for example, is practically a given among many poets. Stafford notes "the importance of just plain receptivity,"[15] and Denise Levertov describes the poet as being "brought to speech" only after a period of quasi-mystical contemplation.[16] The importance of sound, particularly rhythm, at this early stage of writing is another value Roethke shared at times with others. For James Wright a poem begins "with a rhythm and not with an idea,"[17] and Stanley Kunitz's description of his poems' typical origins could apply to much of Roethke's work on *Open House* and parts of *Praise to the End!*:

> Because it *is* a pre-verbal activity, it is very hard to describe it in words! But I suspect that when one detects in oneself this surge of rhythm and counter-rhythm, really what you are locating is a complex of feelings.... It is a complex of thoughts and feelings looking for a language, seeking a language.... But the only way it can shape itself, in the beginning, is in wordless rhythms which gradually attach themselves to words. And then that fog becomes palpable....

[Kunitz's emphasis][18]

A fierce attention to conscious craft once the "fog" has become "palpable" is a common feature in most poets' writing methods. Kunitz notes the "deliberate consciousness" involved in taking a poem from initial handwritten drafts through typed versions,[19] and Robert Lowell, in a remark typical of many poets, speaks of revising "endlessly."[20] As James Wright put it, "Without craft, by which I mean the active employment of the intelligence, the imagination, that mysterious and frightening thing, can not come free."[21]

On the level of general principles, then, the parallels between Roethke's writing methods and those of other modern poets are extensive. But when we consider the specifics of the writing process, the unique variety and intensity of Roethke's work becomes apparent. The poet's notebooks, with fragments of verse, prose, and quotations of other writers; writing in different ink at different times, sometimes directly on top of earlier entries; and erratic dating, circling and crossing over of material in frequent re-readings, are overwhelming in their energy and sheer bulk. William Stafford includes a sample page from his notebook at the end of "A Way of Writing";[22] it looks like a clean finished draft in comparison to Roethke's frenetic efforts. The step-by-step development of Lowell's "breakthrough" poems in *Life Studies,* though it involved such techniques as rewriting prose as poetry and changing poems in rhyme and meter to free verse, is much more organized than Roethke's parallel work in the composition of *The Lost Son and Other Poems.*[23] Even a poet as deeply committed to following intuition in the creative process as Levertov seems more methodical than Roethke as she revises a single poem draft after draft.[24] The differences between Roethke and these other poets are not the result of an inherent sloppiness on Roethke's part; his published work is too carefully wrought for that. Rather, the more unusual compositional techniques Roethke developed at different stages in his career— the obsessive cycle-making, selection of lines out of different contexts, the use of interchangeable lines, the separation of concepts from illustrative description, and the rest—reflect his sense of himself as a "perpetual beginner."

William Stafford concludes "A Way of Writing" with this expansive vision of the writing process:

But writing itself is one of the great, free human activities. There is scope for individuality, and elation, and discovery, in writing. For the person who follows with trust and forgiveness what occurs to him, the world remains always ready and deep, an inexhaustible environment, with the combined vividness of an actuality and flexibility of a dream. Working back and forth between experience and thought, writers have more than space and time can offer. They have the whole unexplored realm of human vision.[25]

Roethke could never have written that statement, just as he could never have sat down calmly to write every morning as Stafford does. Though Roethke certainly found "elation" and "discovery" in writing, as his description of writing "The Dance" in 1952 indicates (SP 23–24), the freedom and ease Stafford notes were something Roethke achieved rarely and only late in his career. Much more common were the anxieties Roethke felt before writing "The Dance": a sense of himself as a fraud and a feeling that he might never be able to write again. Richard Hugo once told me he thought that the frenetic quality of Roethke's work in the notebooks and the poet's habit of scribbling notes for poems on odd slips of paper whenever a line or an idea struck him both stemmed from a deep fear of losing *anything* that might possibly become part of a poem. Roethke found writing difficult and essential at the same time. The unusual compositional techniques he developed are, to some extent, ways to mitigate the difficulties. Rereading notebooks and culling lines from them, for example, removed the pressure of inventing what to write next in a given poem; cycle-making helped light one poem with the dying embers of another, avoiding the terrifying silence between works and the difficulty of starting up again; interchangeable lines guaranteed a supply of usable poetic material. These are the techniques of a man for whom the process of writing was a struggle.

More importantly, however, the unique compositional approaches of the "perpetual beginner" reflect the intensity of his commitment to the task at hand. Roethke might have found writing more easy if he had been content with less. A devotion to artistic craftsmanship is one facet of this commitment. In a letter to Roethke just before the poet's death, another master "craftsman," Robert Lowell, captured this quality: "One of the things I marvel at in your poems is the impression they give of having been worked an extra half day, when another writer would have curled up with exhaustion" (TR 9–12). But for Roethke, as for Lowell and others, aesthetic skill and control did not exist in a vacuum; craft was only a tool, the perfected poem only a part of a larger process. In his letter Lowell compares himself and Roethke with the other poets of their generation, concluding that "to write we seem to have to go at it with such single-minded intensity that we are always on the point of drowning" (TR 9–12). The intensity Lowell notes reflects the deep connection between the process of writing and the self in both Roethke's and Lowell's work. It was this central relation that led to the richness and variety in the different stages of Roethke's career. The poet's former student James Wright sensed this at an important transitional point in his own work. Writing to Roethke in 1958, he noted:

> I've been cracking my own facility, my competence, my dead and dull iambs, to pieces. What makes this so ironically depressing, as I say, is that I am trapped by the very thing—the traditional technique—which I labored so hard to attain. Not till this year did I *really* understand the heroism of your advancing through various stages of style—for style in your work has not been *only* a technical matter, but rather primarily a self-discovery, self-conquest, self-revelation. (TR 15–7, Wright's emphasis)

We can look at Roethke's career as a series of "traps" like the one Wright describes; each kind of poem Roethke wrote gradually revealed its limitations as the poet developed its strengths. That Roethke was able to see these traps and break again and again into new work shows his dedication and skill as a poet. It also shows his courage, as Wright notes. In progressing from self-creation, through self-discovery, to the "long journey out of the self," Roethke forged a complex and dynamic relation between personal identity and the writing process. The strength of his work is rooted in this convergence of life and art.

Notes

NOTES TO CHAPTER 1

1. Theodore Roethke, *Straw for the Fire: From the Notebooks of Theodore Roethke, 1943–1963*, ed. David Wagoner (Garden City, New York: Doubleday, 1972), 150.
2. Richard Howard, *Alone with America: Essays on the Art of Poetry in the United States Since 1950* (New York: Atheneum, 1971), xiii.
3. Richard Allen Blessing, *Theodore Roethke's Dynamic Vision* (Bloomington: Indiana University Press, 1974), 3.
4. Yeats' journal is included in his *Memoirs*, Denis Donoghue, ed. (New York: Macmillan, 1972). The quotation is from "Discoveries" in Yeats' *Essays and Introductions* (New York: Macmillan, 1961), 272.
5. Unless otherwise noted, biographical information in this book is from Allan Seager's *The Glass House: The Life of Theodore Roethke* (New York: McGraw-Hill, 1968) and the poet's own correspondence and notebooks.
6. Publication dates and other bibliographical information in this book are from Keith R. Moul's *Theodore Roethke's Career: An Annotated Bibliography* (Boston: G.K. Hall, 1977), unless otherwise noted.
7. All material in the Theodore Roethke Papers is copyright Mrs. Beatrice Roethke Lushington and can be reprinted only with her permission. For clarity in quoting draft and notebook material, I have deleted material not pertinent to the discussion and omitted the lines and passages crossed out by the poet, except when they are particularly relevant. I have corrected obvious typographical errors and retained Roethke's punctuation. Notebook numbers were not assigned by the poet and do not necessarily indicate the order of their composition.

NOTES TO CHAPTER 2

1. Blessing, 41.
2. Rolfe Humphries, "Inside Story," review of *Open House, The New Republic*, 14 July 1941, 62.
3. Ralph J. Mills, Jr., *Theodore Roethke* (Minneapolis: University of Minnesota Press, 1963), 9.
4. Louis Martz, "A Greenhouse Eden," in *Theodore Roethke: Essays on the Poetry*, ed. Arnold Stein (Seattle: University of Washington Press, 1965), 18–19.
5. W.H. Auden, "Verse and the Times," review of *Open House, Saturday Review*, 5 April 1941, 30.
6. William Meredith, "A Steady Stream of Correspondences: Theodore Roethke's Long Journey Out of the Self," in *Theodore Roethke: Essays on the*

Poetry, 38.

7. Louise Bogan, introduction to a selection of Roethke's work, in *Trial Balances*, ed. Ann Winslow (New York: Macmillan, 1935), 138.

8. John Holmes, review of *Open House, Boston Evening Transcript*, 24 March 1941, 9.

9. Karl Malkoff, *Theodore Roethke: An Introduction to the Poetry* (New York: Columbia University Press, 1966), 32–33.

10. Ibid., 28.

11. The manuscript was rejected by Yale University Press, Macmillan, Oxford University Press, and Henry Holt and Company, in that order.

12. Unless otherwise noted, the excluded poems discussed in this chapter are from *Poems of Theodore Roethke* (TR 26–1).

13. "This Light" appeared in *American Poetry Journal* 17 (November 1934), 3; "The Buds Now Stretch" was published in *The New York Times*, 9 November 1938, 22.

14. *The New Republic*, 20 December 1939, 254.

15. Jenijoy La Belle, *The Echoing Wood of Theodore Roethke* (Princeton: Princeton University Press, 1976), 17.

16. Gerard Manley Hopkins, "Pied Beauty," in *Poems and Prose of Gerard Manley Hopkins*, ed. W.H. Gardner (Baltimore: Penguin, 1953), 31.

17. La Belle, 7.

18. Rosemary Sullivan, *Theodore Roethke: The Garden Master* (Seattle: University of Washington Press, 1975), 5.

19. Both poems appeared in *The New Yorker:* "Lines upon Leaving a Sanitarium" in 13 April 1937, 30; and "Meditation in Hydrotherapy" in 15 May 1937, 87. Both are reprinted in Roethke's *Collected Poems*, 256–57.

20. James Richard McLeod, *Theodore Roethke: A Manuscript Checklist* (Oberlin: Kent State University Press, 1971), 66.

21. Blessing, 31.

22. Louis Martz, 22.

23. Auden, review of *Open House*, 30.

NOTES TO CHAPTER 3

1. Mills, *Theodore Roethke*, 11.

2. Stephen Spender, "The Objective Ego," in *Theodore Roethke: Essays on the Poetry*, 8.

3. Kenneth Burke, "Cult of the Breakthrough," review of *Selected Letters of Theodore Roethke, The New Republic*, 21 September 1968, 25.

4. Mills, *Theodore Roethke*, 11.

5. For more on the concept of the core of identity, see Mary R. Hayden,

"*Open House:* Poetry of the Constricted Self," *Northwest Review* 11 (Summer 1971), 116–38.

6. Auden, review of *Open House*, 30.

7. This text is reproduced in Roethke's essay "Verse in Rehearsal" in *On the Poet and His Craft*, 32.

8. On the draft he sent to Humphries, Roethke noted that the poem had been rejected by *The Nation, Virginia Quarterly Review,* and *Saturday Review.*

9. Versions of these poems are included in Roethke's *Selected Letters,* 10, 24.

10. Dennis E. Brown, "Theodore Roethke's 'Self-World' and the Modernist Position," *Journal of Modern Literature* 3 (July 1974), 1243.

11. Blessing, 65.

12. An earlier version of this stanza is reprinted in Roethke's *Selected Letters,* 76.

13. Robert Lowell, interviewed by Frederick Seidel, in *Writers at Work: The Paris Review Interviews,* Second Series (New York: Viking, 1963), 346.

14. For more on the role of William Carlos Williams in Roethke's breakthrough, see Peter Balakian, "Theodore Roethke, William Carlos Williams and the American Grain," *Modern Language Studies* 17 (Winter 1987), 54–66.

15. Seager, 160–64. Some examples of Seager's exaggeration are his statement that in the early notebooks Roethke worked on only one poem at a time, his finding that the early notebooks contained almost nothing but poetry, and his description of these notebooks as "always dead serious." My own examination of all the notebooks from 1930 through 1945 supports none of these conclusions.

16. A version of this interview, edited by Neal Bowers, was published in *New Letters* 49 (Fall 1982), 4–25. Roethke also refers to Rilkean "looking" in the symposium "On 'Identity' " in *On the Poet and His Craft.*

17. Jay Parini, *Theodore Roethke: An American Romantic* (Amherst: University of Massachusetts Press, 1979), 70.

18. Arnold Stein, "Roethke's Memory: Actions, Visions, and Revisions," *Northwest Review* 11 (Summer 1971), 28.

19. Jarold Ramsey, "Roethke in the Greenhouse," *Western Humanities Review* 26 (Winter 1972), 40.

NOTES TO CHAPTER 4

1. Blessing notes the movement toward meditation, 77; the "general sense of growth" is from Malkoff, 50; and the progression toward transcendence is from Sullivan, 26.

2. The cinematic metaphor is a natural one for Roethke's vivid work, and Parini (73) compares the greenhouse poems to films, in contrast to the still photos of *Open House*. Certainly there is more movement in the greenhouse poems than in Roethke's earlier work, but I am thinking more of the nature of film as a sequential medium. The greenhouse poems could be seen as individual "short subjects," but they do not make a complete "movie" in the way the later sequences do.

3. Seager, 156. Though Roethke's technique of composing longer poems from fragments written at different times makes it impossible to discover exact dates of composition, the approximate date when a poem was completed can often be determined. In making these determinations, I have relied on evidence from *The Glass House,* the poet's letters, and Moul's bibliography.

4. Louis Martz, 33.

5. Roethke, *Straw for the Fire,* 149–51.

6. Sullivan, 9–14.

7. Seager, 85. This particular image of the poet raises important political issues about the artist, audience, and society. For an excellent study of these issues see Denise Levertov's article on Anne Sexton, "Light Up the Cave," *Ramparts,* December 1974–January 1975, 61–63.

8. Seager, 288–89.

9. Kenneth Burke, "The Vegetal Radicalism of Theodore Roethke," *Sewanee Review* 58 (Winter 1950), 86.

10. Louis Martz, 31.

11. There are tapes of this reading at radio station KPFA in Berkeley, California, and at the University of Washington library.

12. Seager, 187.

13. Burke, "Vegetal Radicalism," 105.

14. Roethke, *Straw for the Fire,* 182.

15. The poem "O, Thou Opening, O," which concludes the volume as it is printed in *Words for the Wind,* was not included in the *Praise to the End!* group until the publication of *The Waking* in 1953. Though superficially resembling the *Praise to the End!* poems in style and structure, "O, Thou Opening, O" was written considerably later than they were; Roethke mentioned it in a letter to Kenneth Burke in late 1952 with no reference to it being part of the sequence (SL 181). Though Rosemary Sullivan reads this poem as a "coda or synopsis" of the sequence (76), it is neither. As Sullivan herself points out, the poem was added to the *Praise to the End!* section in *The Waking* "almost as an afterthought" (76). It is clear that the work was not an intrinsic part of *Praise to the End!* as Roethke was writing it. In *The Collected Poems of Theodore Roethke* it has been removed from the *Praise to the End!* section and placed with the later *Waking* poems, where it belongs.

16. For a thorough study of the parallels between Roethke's "tensed-up *Prelude"* and the original, see La Belle, 43–50.
17. William Wordsworth, *The Prelude: A Parallel Text,* ed. J.C. Maxwell (Baltimore: Penguin, 1971), 55.
18. Roethke, "Give Way, Ye Gates," *Botteghe Oscure* 6 (1950), 449.
19. Blessing, 115.
20. Malkoff, 104.

NOTES TO CHAPTER 5

1. Seager, 161.
2. For more on Roethke's use of such primitive, associative language, see Blessing, 94–96.
3. The panel, entitled "Theodore Roethke: The Teaching Poet," took place at the 1979 Modern Language Association Convention in San Francisco. Members included Tess Gallagher, Richard Hugo, Jenijoy La Belle and Arnold Stein; I served as moderator. Tess Gallagher's remarks from the panel were published in *The American Poetry Review* 9 (March– April 1980), 38–39.
4. Meredith, 41.
5. Blessing, 95.
6. James Wright, interviewed by Peter Stitt, *The Paris Review* 62 (Summer 1975), 42.

NOTES TO CHAPTER 6

1. Coburn Freer, "Theodore Roethke's Love Poetry," *Northwest Review* 11 (Summer 1971), 42–43.
2. Stanley Kunitz, "News of the Root," review of *The Lost Son and Other Poems, Poetry* 73 (January 1949), 225.
3. Stephen Spender, "Roethke: The Lost Son," review of *The Collected Poems of Theodore Roethke, The New Republic,* 27 August 1966, 23.
4. Thom Gunn, "Poets English and American," review of *Words for the Wind, The Yale Review* 48 (June 1959), 624.
5. La Belle, 117.
6. Richard Hugo, *The Triggering Town* (New York: Norton, 1979), 31.
7. Ibid.
8. Auden defines the role of form in the writing process in "Writing," in *The Dyer's Hand and Other Essays* (New York: Random House, 1962), 22; and "Pope," in *From Anne to Victoria: Essays by Various Hands,* ed. Bonamy Dobrée (New York: Scribner's, 1937), 100.
9. Robert Conquest, "The Language of Men," review of *Words for the*

Wind, The Spectator, 14 February 1958, 210–11.

10. William J. Martz, ed., *The Achievement of Theodore Roethke* (Glenview, Illinois: Scott, Foresman, 1966), 11–12.

11. Blessing, 179.

12. Roethke, "Words for the Wind," in *Poet's Choice,* ed. Paul Engle and Joseph Langland (New York: Dell, 1962), 100. For more on the technical devices which create the "swiftness" here, see Blessing, 175–77.

13. Roethke, "Words for the Wind," in *Poet's Choice,* 99.

14. John Crowe Ransom, comments on Theodore Roethke's "In a Dark Time," in *The Contemporary Poet as Artist and Critic,* ed. Anthony Ostroff (Boston: Little, Brown and Company, 1964), 29; Frederick J. Hoffman, "Theodore Roethke: The Poetic Shape of Death," in *Theodore Roethke: Essays on the Poetry,* 106–8.

15. Roethke, comments on "In a Dark Time," in *The Contemporary Poet as Artist and Critic,* 52.

16. Drawing on the mystic tradition of parallels between erotic and divine love, Neal Bowers develops an interesting reading of metaphysical issues in the love poems themselves in *Theodore Roethke: The Journey from I to Otherwise* (Columbia: University of Missouri Press, 1982), 120–45.

17. The quotations from Freer in this and the following paragraph are from pp. 62–64.

NOTES TO CHAPTER 7

1. Seamus Heaney, "Canticles to the Earth," review of *The Collected Poems of Theodore Roethke, The Listener,* 22 August 1968, 245.

2. "Circling" is from Sullivan, 133; "resonating" is from Harry Williams, *"The Edge Is What I Have": Theodore Roethke and After* (Lewisburg: Bucknell University Press, 1977), 99; and "rocking" is from Stanley Kunitz, "Roethke: Poet of Transformations," *The New Republic,* 23 January 1965, 26.

3. Malkoff, 164.

4. Burke, "Vegetal Radicalism," 107–8.

5. Parini, 158.

6. John Wain, "The Monocle of My Sea-Faced Uncle," in *Theodore Roethke: Essays on the Poetry,* 67–68.

7. Hugh Staples, "The Rose in the Sea-Wind: A Reading of Theodore Roethke's 'North American Sequence,'" *American Literature* 36 (May 1964), 189–90.

8. Malkoff, 177.

9. Sullivan, 157.

10. James McMichael, "The Poetry of Theodore Roethke," *The Southern Review* New Series 5 (Winter 1969), 18–20.

11. Staples, 199.

12. "Journey to the Interior" first appeared in *The New Yorker*, 7 January 1961, 27.

13. Staples, 199–200.

14. Ralph J. Mills, Jr., "In the Way of Becoming: Roethke's Last Poems," in *Theodore Roethke: Essays on the Poetry*, 124.

15. Harry Williams, 108.

16. Sullivan, 163.

17. Louis Martz, 22.

18. La Belle, 158.

19. Thomas Gardner's " 'North American Sequence' and the American Long Poem," in *Theodore Roethke*, ed. Harold Bloom (New York: Chelsea House, 1988), 177–94, notes some intriguing antecedents for Roethke's conclusions here in Whitman's "Song of Myself" as well as parallels in long poems by Roethke's contemporaries.

20. Heaney, 245.

NOTES TO CHAPTER 8

1. Roethke also considered *O, Motion, O* (from "The Motion," 4. 6) and *Once More, the Round* as titles for the volume (TR 17–17, 27–16), but *Dance On, Dance On, Dance On* remained his first choice from early 1962 through mid-March of the following year (TR 17–17, 17–29).

2. La Belle, 168; Roy Harvey Pearce, "Theodore Roethke: The Power of Sympathy," in *Theodore Roethke: Essays on the Poetry*, 197–99.

3. Seager, 279.

4. Hugo, 73.

5. La Belle, 166.

6. T.S. Eliot, "Tradition and the Individual Talent," in *The Sacred Wood* (London: Methuen, 1928), 58.

7. Ibid., 52–53.

8. Eliot, "Little Gidding," in *The Complete Poems and Plays, 1909–1950* (New York: Harcourt, Brace & World, 1962), 145.

9. See M.L. Rosenthal, *The New Poets: American and British Poetry Since World War II* (New York: Oxford University Press, 1967), 112–18, and Robert Phillips, *The Confessional Poets* (Carbondale: Southern Illinois University Press, 1973), 107–27. It is significant that both critics find fault with Roethke's vision of transcendence. Regardless of whether this vision is believable or not, the fact that Roethke strives for self-transcendence belies the characterization of him as confessional. A true confessional poet—Robert Lowell, for example—might work toward a cathartic escape from anxieties, but an actual transcendence of the limits of identity would not be a goal or even

a possibility, except in the negative sense of a nervous breakdown. In confessional poetry the self is exposed and then "healed" in the psychoanalytic model of catharsis; it is not transcended.

10. Phillips, 126. "Lines upon Leaving a Sanitarium" and "Meditation in Hydrotherapy" both appeared in *The New Yorker* in 1937, the former in the March 13th issue, p. 30, and the latter in the May 15th issue, p. 87. "Heard in a Violent Ward," also mentioned by Phillips as a "late" poem, appeared in *Poetry* 77 (February 1951), 262.

11. Hugo, 72.

12. Eliot, "Tradition and the Individual Talent," 59.

13. Hugo, 73–74.

14. William Stafford, "A Way of Writing," in *A Field Guide to Contemporary Poetry and Poetics,* ed. Stuart Friebert and David Young (New York: Longman, 1980), 1.

15. Ibid.

16. Denise Levertov, "Some Notes on Organic Form," in *Naked Poetry: Recent American Poetry in Open Forms,* ed. Stephen Berg and Robert Mezey (New York: Bobbs-Merrill, 1969), 141–42.

17. Wright, 54.

18. Stanley Kunitz, "Action and Incantation," an interview with Harvey Gross, *Antaeus* 30–31 (Spring 1978), 284. I have deleted the interviewer's question in the middle of the quotation and one of Kunitz's remarks, but the ellipsis at the end is Kunitz's own.

19. Kunitz, "Action and Incantation," 291–93.

20. Lowell, 350.

21. Wright, 58.

22. Stafford, 5.

23. The information on Lowell's compositional methods for *Life Studies* is from Steven Gould Axelrod, *Robert Lowell: Life and Art* (Princeton: Princeton University Press, 1978), 107–21. Axelrod includes some revealing drafts of Lowell's poems in Appendix B, 247–50.

24. Levertov discusses the composition of three poems in "Work and Inspiration: Inviting the Muse," in *A Field Guide to Contemporary Poetry and Poetics,* 8–24. *Fifty Contemporary Poets: The Creative Process,* ed. Alberta T. Turner (New York: Longman, 1977) includes manuscripts and comments on the writing process by Levertov (193–201) and others.

25. Stafford, 4.

List of Works Cited

Works by Theodore Roethke

Unpublished Material:
The Theodore Roethke Papers. Suzallo Library, University of Washington, Seattle.

Poetry:
Open House. New York: Alfred A. Knopf, 1941.
The Lost Son and Other Poems. Garden City, New York: Doubleday, 1948.
Praise to the End! Garden City, New York: Doubleday, 1951.
The Waking: Poems 1933-1953. Garden City, New York: Doubleday, 1954.
Words for the Wind. London: Secker & Warburg, 1957; Garden City, New York: Doubleday, 1958.
The Far Field. Garden City, New York: Doubleday, 1964.
The Collected Poems of Theodore Roethke. Garden City, New York: Doubleday, 1966.

Prose:
Comments on "In a Dark Time." In *The Contemporary Poet as Artist and Critic*. Ed. Anthony Ostroff. Boston: Little, Brown, 1964.
Comments on "Words for the Wind." In *Poet's Choice*. Ed. Paul Engle and Joseph Langland. New York: Dell, 1962.
Note to "Give Way, Ye Gates." *Botteghe Oscure* 6 (1950): 449.
On the Poet and His Craft: Selected Prose of Theodore Roethke. Ed. Ralph J. Mills, Jr. Seattle: University of Washington Press, 1965.
Selected Letters of Theodore Roethke. Ed. Ralph J. Mills, Jr. Seattle: University of Washington Press, 1968.
Straw for the Fire: From the Notebooks of Theodore Roethke, 1943-1963. Ed. David Wagoner. Garden City, New York: Doubleday, 1972.

Works by Other Authors

Auden, W.H. *The Dyer's Hand and Other Essays*. New York: Random House, 1962.

_____. "Pope." In *From Anne to Victoria: Essays by Various Hands*. Ed. Bonamy Dobrée. New York: Scribner's, 1937.

_____. "Verse and the Times." Review of *Open House*, by Theodore Roethke. *Saturday Review*, 5 April 1941, 30–31.

Axelrod, Steven Gould. *Robert Lowell: Life and Art*. Princeton: Princeton University Press, 1978.

Balakian, Peter. "Theodore Roethke, William Carlos Williams and the American Grain." *Modern Language Studies* 17 (Winter 1987): 54–66.

Blessing, Richard Allen. *Theodore Roethke's Dynamic Vision*. Bloomington: Indiana University Press, 1974.

Bogan, Louise. Introduction to a Selection of Poems by Theodore Roethke. In *Trial Balances*. Ed. Ann Winslow. New York: Macmillan, 1935.

Bowers, Neal. *Theodore Roethke: The Journey from I to Otherwise*. Columbia: University of Missouri Press, 1982.

Brown, Dennis E. "Theodore Roethke's 'Self-World' and the Modernist Position." *Journal of Modern Literature* 3 (July 1974): 1239–54.

Burke, Kenneth. "Cult of the Breakthrough." Review of *Selected Letters of Theodore Roethke*. *The New Republic*, 21 September 1968, 25–26.

_____. "The Vegetal Radicalism of Theodore Roethke." *Sewanee Review* 58 (Winter 1950): 68–108.

Conquest, Robert. "The Language of Men." Review of *Words for the Wind*, by Theodore Roethke. *The Spectator*, 14 February 1958, 210–11.

Eliot, T.S. "Little Gidding." In *The Complete Poems and Plays, 1909–1950*. New York: Harcourt, Brace & World, 1962.

_____. "Tradition and the Individual Talent." In *The Sacred Wood*. London: Methuen, 1928.

Freer, Coburn. "Theodore Roethke's Love Poetry." *Northwest Review* 11 (Summer 1971): 42–66.

Gallagher, Tess. "Last Class with Roethke." *The American Poetry Review* 9 (March–April 1980): 38–39.

Gardner, Thomas. " 'North American Sequence' and the American Long Poem." In *Theodore Roethke*. Ed. Harold Bloom. New York: Chelsea House, 1988.

Gunn, Thom. "Poets English and American." Review of *Words for the Wind,* by Theodore Roethke. *The Yale Review* 48 (June 1959): 623–25.

Hayden, Mary R. *"Open House:* Poetry of the Constricted Self." *Northwest Review* 11 (Summer 1971): 116–38.

Heaney, Seamus. "Canticles to the Earth." Review of *The Collected Poems of Theodore Roethke. The Listener,* 22 August 1968, 245–46.

Hoffman, Frederick J. "Theodore Roethke: The Poetic Shape of Death." In *Theodore Roethke: Essays on the Poetry.* Ed. Arnold Stein. Seattle: University of Washington Press, 1965.

Holmes, John. Review of *Open House,* by Theodore Roethke. *Boston Evening Transcript,* 24 March 1941, 9.

Hopkins, Gerard Manley. "Pied Beauty." In *Poems and Prose of Gerard Manley Hopkins.* Ed. W.H. Gardner. Baltimore: Penguin, 1953.

Howard, Richard. *Alone with America: Essays on the Art of Poetry in the United States Since 1950.* New York: Atheneum, 1971.

Hugo, Richard. *The Triggering Town.* New York: Norton, 1979.

Humphries, Rolfe. "Inside Story." Review of *Open House,* by Theodore Roethke. *The New Republic,* 14 July 1941, 62.

Kunitz, Stanley. "Action and Incantation." Interview with Harvey Gross. *Antaeus* 30–31 (Spring 1978): 283–95.

———. "News of the Root." Review of *The Lost Son and Other Poems,* by Theodore Roethke. *Poetry* 73 (January 1949): 222–25.

———. "Roethke: Poet of Transformations." *The New Republic,* 23 January 1965, 23–29.

La Belle, Jenijoy. *The Echoing Wood of Theodore Roethke.* Princeton: Princeton University Press, 1976.

Levertov, Denise. Comments on the Writing of "The 90th Year." In *Fifty Contemporary Poets: The Creative Process.* Ed. Alberta T. Turner. New York: Longman, 1977.

———. "Light Up the Cave." *Ramparts,* December 1974–January 1975, 61–63.

———. "Some Notes on Organic Form." In *Naked Poetry: Recent American Poetry in Open Forms.* Ed. Stephen Berg and Robert Mezey. New York: Bobbs-Merrill, 1969.

———. "Work and Inspiration: Inviting the Muse." In *A Field*

Guide to Contemporary Poetry and Poetics. Ed. Stuart
Friebert and David Young. New York: Longman, 1980.
Lowell, Robert. Interview with Frederick Seidel. In *Writers at Work:
The Paris Review Interviews.* 2nd Series. New York: Viking, 1963.
Malkoff, Karl. *Theodore Roethke: An Introduction to the Poetry.*
New York: Columbia University Press, 1966.
Martz, Louis. "A Greenhouse Eden." In *Theodore Roethke: Essays on
the Poetry.* Ed. Arnold Stein. Seattle: University of Washington Press, 1965.
Martz, William J., ed. *The Achievement of Theodore Roethke.* Glenview, Illinois: Scott, Foresman, 1966.
McLeod, James Richard. *Theodore Roethke: A Manuscript Checklist.*
Oberlin: Kent State University Press, 1971.
McMichael, James. "The Poetry of Theodore Roethke." *The Southern
Review* New Series 5 (Winter 1969): 4–25.
Meredith, William. "A Steady Stream of Correspondences: Theodore
Roethke's Long Journey Out of the Self." In *Theodore
Roethke: Essays on the Poetry.* Ed. Arnold Stein. Seattle:
University of Washington Press, 1965.
Mills, Ralph J., Jr. "In the Way of Becoming: Roethke's Last
Poems." In *Theodore Roethke: Essays on the Poetry.* Ed.
Arnold Stein. Seattle: University of Washington Press,
1965.
———. *Theodore Roethke.* Minneapolis: University of Minnesota
Press, 1963.
Moul, Keith R. *Theodore Roethke's Career: An Annotated Bibliography.* Boston: G.K. Hall, 1977.
Parini, Jay. *Theodore Roethke: An American Romantic.* Amherst:
University of Massachusetts Press, 1979.
Pearce, Roy Harvey. "Theodore Roethke: The Power of Sympathy."
In *Theodore Roethke: Essays on the Poetry.* Ed. Arnold
Stein. Seattle: University of Washington Press, 1965.
Phillips, Robert. *The Confessional Poets.* Carbondale: Southern Illinois University Press, 1973.
Ramsey, Jarold. "Roethke in the Greenhouse." *Western Humanities
Review* 26 (Winter 1972): 35–47.
Ransom, John Crowe. Comments on "In a Dark Time," by Theodore
Roethke. In *The Contemporary Poet as Artist and Critic.* Ed.

Anthony Ostroff. Boston: Little, Brown, 1964.

Rosenthal, M.L. *The New Poets: American and British Poetry Since World War II*. New York: Oxford University Press, 1967.

Seager, Allan. *The Glass House: The Life of Theodore Roethke*. New York: McGraw-Hill, 1968.

Spender, Stephen. "The Objective Ego." In *Theodore Roethke: Essays on the Poetry*. Ed. Arnold Stein. Seattle: University of Washington Press, 1965.

————. "Roethke: The Lost Son." Review of *The Collected Poems of Theodore Roethke*. *The New Republic*, 27 August 1966, 23–25.

Stafford, William. "A Way of Writing." In *A Field Guide to Contemporary Poetry and Poetics*. Ed. Stuart Friebert and David Young. New York: Longman, 1980.

Staples, Hugh. "The Rose in the Sea-Wind: A Reading of Theodore Roethke's 'North American Sequence.' " *American Literature* 36 (May 1964): 189–203.

Stein, Arnold. "Roethke's Memory: Actions, Visions, and Revisions." *Northwest Review* 11 (Summer 1971): 19–31.

————, ed. *Theodore Roethke: Essays on the Poetry*. Seattle: University of Washington Press, 1965.

Sullivan, Rosemary. *Theodore Roethke: The Garden Master*. Seattle: University of Washington Press, 1975.

Wain, John. "The Monocle of My Sea-Faced Uncle." In *Theodore Roethke: Essays on the Poetry*. Ed. Arnold Stein. Seattle: University of Washington Press, 1965.

Williams, Harry. *"The Edge Is What I Have": Theodore Roethke and After*. Lewisburg: Bucknell University Press, 1977.

Wordsworth, William. *The Prelude: A Parallel Text*. Ed. J.C. Maxwell. Baltimore: Penguin, 1971.

Wright, James. Interview with Peter Stitt. *The Paris Review* 62 (Summer 1975): 34–61.

Yeats, W.B. *Essays and Introductions*. New York: Macmillan, 1961.

————. *Memoirs*. Ed. Denis Donoghue. New York: Macmillan, 1972.

Index

Wagoner, David, 87
Wain, John, 144, 147
"The Waking," 172
The Waking, 4, 101, 179n. 15; notebook work for, 104–11
"Weed Puller," 45, 46, 49–50, 55
"We Sighed for a Sign," 24
"What Can I Tell My Bones?," 135, 136, 139, 145, 171
"Where Knock Is Open Wide," 69, 137; arrangement of material in drafts, 93–98; composition of, 75–99; cyclic progress in, 98; as first poem of "tensed-up *Prelude*," 68, 78; generation of notebook material, 79–86; and narrative, 84–86, 89; and nonsense verse, 82–83; and *The Prelude*, 79; Roethke's comments on draft sheets, 93–95; selection of material from notebooks, 86–93
Whitman, Walt, 146, 148, 182n. 19
Williams, Harry, 134, 159, 181n. 2
Williams, William Carlos, 43, 49, 143, 178n. 14
Winters, Yvor, 44
"Wish for a Young Wife," 132
"Words for the Wind," 121–22, 124, 125, 126, 132; rhyme in, 121–22, 131; trimeter in, 121
Words for the Wind, 4, 100–1, 123–24, 131, 134, 155, 167, 179n. 15; inductive approach in, 155; and "Love Poems" in Part II of *The Far Field*, 125–28; notebook work for, 104–11, 138–42; pentameter and trimeter in, 121–22
Wordsworth, William: *The Prelude*, 68–69, 72, 79, 159, 179–80n. 16
"The Wraith," 107, 110–11; semicolons in, 108
Wright, James, 98, 172–73, 175
Wylie, Elinor, 19

Yeats, W.B., 2, 101, 103–4
"The Young Girl," 126–28
"Young Girl's Songs": early title for love "songs," 126

A NOTE ABOUT THE AUTHOR

Don Bogen did undergraduate and graduate work at the University of California, Berkeley, and is currently Associate Professor of English at the University of Cincinnati. The author of a book of poetry, *After the Splendid Display* (Wesleyan University Press, 1986), he has received grants for his work from the Ingram Merrill Foundation and the National Endowment for the Arts. His critical essays and reviews have appeared in *English Literary History, The Nation* and other journals.